Awaken to Healing

Reclaiming Power and Peace Through Past Life Regression

Jaya Kalra

DEDICATION

I lovingly dedicate this book to my beloved father, the late Shree S.R. Ghai, my cherished mother, the late Smt. Sushma Ghai, and my dear daughter, the late Dr. Rachita Kalra. Their divine inspiration and spiritual guidance have been my constant companions, urging me forward with every word written. This book would not have been possible without their love, wisdom, and the light they continue to shine on my path. Their blessings are woven into every page, forever close to my heart.

Contents

Jaya Kalra

ACKNOWLEDGMENTS

As I sit down to reflect on the journey of bringing this book to life, my heart is filled with immense gratitude for the support and encouragement that surrounded me.

First and foremost, I owe a deep thanks to my husband, Rajiv, my son, Aneesh, and my daughter-in-law, Pratibha, for giving me the space, love, and understanding that allowed my creativity to flow freely. Without their unwavering support and the nurturing environment they created, this book would not have been possible.

To my teachers – Dr. Newton Kondaveti, Dr. Lakshmi, Dr. N.K. Sharma, and Savita Sharma – your teachings and wisdom have left an indelible mark on me, shaping both my life and this work in profound ways. You are the guiding lights that have inspired me beyond measure.

A special thank you goes to Sweta Samota, a talented author and the owner of India Authors Academy. Her gentle push and invaluable guidance helped me stay disciplined and determined to complete this book on time. I truly appreciate your belief in me, Sweta, and your encouragement every step of the way.

Lastly, I would like to extend my heartfelt thanks to my manager, Divakar Pandey, for his timely and untimely assistance, always there when I needed it most.

Each one of you has played a vital role in this journey, and I carry your contributions and love in every page of this book. Thank you, from the bottom of my heart.

FOREWARD

In a world that often feels fragmented, as we search for wholeness and healing, we find ourselves drawn to ancient wisdom, inner journeys, and profound self-discovery. *Awaken to Healing: Reclaiming Power and Peace through Past Life Regression* is a guide to unlock deeper understanding of ourselves, both in this life and beyond. This book guides us to reclaim the peace and power to attain balance through holistic healing techniques. As an Ayurvedic practitioner, I have witnessed the profound impact of ancient healing techniques on the mind, body, and soul. This book provides a remarkable blend of these age-old principles with modern self-discovery practices, inviting readers to venture within and heal from past traumas and negative experiences.

Awaken to Healing book explores the potential of past life regression—a tool not only for understanding the past but also for transforming the present. By revisiting memories and experiences across lifetimes, we can confront and heal the echoes of trauma, fears, and limitations that may be lingering in our current lives.

The insights shared here are both practical and deeply compassionate, making this book a guide for beginners and experienced seekers alike. With clear instructions, *Awaken to Healing* serves as a safe and supportive roadmap for anyone ready to explore the layers of their soul's journey. Whether you are approaching this book with curiosity, doubt, or a yearning for change, you will find that it invites you gently yet firmly into a space of acceptance and discovery.

Jaya Kalra, the author of the book, has crafted a journey through past life regression, Reiki, inner healing, and more, offering practical insights and accessible methods. This book is a gift—a stepping stone on the path to true healing and self-realization. May this book be your companion on this transformative journey, helping you to reclaim your power, find your peace, and awaken to the vast possibilities that lie within. Welcome to a journey that transcends time and brings you back to the essence of who you truly are.

Dr. Partap Chauhan
Director, Jiva Ayurveda
Delhi. November, 2024.

INTRODUCTION

This book you hold in your hands is not just a collection of chapters or a series of techniques—it is a doorway. A doorway to a journey that will take you deeper into yourself than you may have ever gone before. I want you to know from the very start that this journey isn't just about healing wounds from the past, nor is it simply about overcoming the challenges life has thrown your way. This journey is about rediscovering who you truly are beneath the layers of pain, conditioning, and societal expectations. It's about gaining back your power, your light, and your authentic self.

Before you dive into these pages, I ask you to pause for a moment. Close your eyes. Take a deep breath. What brought you here? Maybe it was a need for healing. Maybe you're tired of feeling stuck, or maybe there's something deep within you longing for change, for freedom. Whatever it is, trust that you're in the right place. This book is a safe space for you to explore those feelings, to reflect, and to grow. You are not alone on this journey. Together, we will walk through every challenge, every emotion, and every realization that unfolds.

As you begin this journey, know that it's okay to feel vulnerable. It's okay to feel uncertain or even resistant. Healing is not always easy, but it is always worth it. Each chapter will guide you through a process—sometimes gently, sometimes intensely—but always with the goal of bringing you closer to your truth, to your wholeness. I invite you to open yourself up to this process, to allow yourself to feel, to heal, and to transform.

Throughout these pages, I will share with you the insights I've gained through my own journey of healing and self-discovery. I've poured my heart into this book, drawing from the lessons life has taught me, and the wisdom I've gathered through helping others heal. You will find stories, practical tools, and spiritual guidance here, all woven together to support you on your unique path.

But this book is not just about me—it's about you. It's about your growth, your evolution, and the steps you are now ready to take. So, as you turn each page, take your time. Reflect on the words. Let them sink in. Trust the process. Trust yourself. Healing doesn't happen overnight, but with patience and persistence, it does happen. There will be moments as you read when things might feel heavy. Old memories may surface, emotions you've buried may come to light. When that happens, take a pause. Breathe through it. Know that these moments are part of the process, and they are here to show you what still needs healing. Be gentle with yourself, but don't shy away from the pain. On the other side of it is the freedom you seek.

This book is more than a guide—it's a companion. I will be here with you, through every chapter, encouraging you to keep going. And when you've reached the end of this book, know that your journey has only just begun. Healing is a lifelong process, but every step you take brings you closer to the life you truly deserve—a life of joy, peace, fulfillment, and self-love.

So, my dear reader, I invite you to step in. With an

open heart and an open mind, allow this journey to transform you in ways you never thought possible.

The time has come for you to embrace your healing, to reclaim your power, and to step fully into the light of who you are meant to be.

Let's begin this journey together.

1. FROM GRIEF TO SPIRITUAL AWAKENING

"The only journey is the one within."
- Rainer Maria Rilke

They say that sometimes, in the quietest moments, the universe whispers to you—soft, barely audible, like the rustling of leaves in the breeze. It was on an ordinary day, in the most unexpected place, that I heard it. It wasn't the universe this time, though. It was my father's voice, clear as day, though he had long since left this world.

I wasn't prepared for what came next. How could I be? Moments like these are not written in books or foretold by anyone. They simply happen, catching you off guard, and changing everything you thought you knew. As I sat waiting for a flight, a door I never knew existed began to open—leading me to places I didn't understand, but somehow, I felt I belonged.

And this is where my journey begins, in the space between what we see and what we sense, between the world we know and the one we are yet to discover.

I will take you deeply into my journey sharing with you how past life regression changed my life along with other techniques that also helped me to come out from depression, anxiety, and negativity.

Like many others, I too tried many conventional methods and medicines, but none helped me come out of it. It was when I accidentally experienced Past Life Regression during my meditation that I ultimately headed towards the path of healing my own life.

The primary focus of this chapter is to connect with you, the reader, by sharing my personal story of struggle and triumphs. Through my experience, I want to help you understand that healing is possible, no matter how overwhelming lifes' challenges may seem. I am not an exception. The transformation I experienced can be accessible to anyone willing to explore the deeper layers of their existence.

I will describe My Battle with its mental and emotional pains – moments where my life felt out of control and darkness overshadowed my every joy. At the time I didn't realize that my present suffering was deep rooted in unresolved issues from past life. When I began my journey with past life regression I found the clarity, peace, and emotional release I had been searching for.

I will take you to the first emotional moment that I experienced. As I encountered past life regression, the doubts I had gradually resolved by profound healing changes that followed. You will see how this healing practice not only helped me identify the source of my inner turmoil but also allowed me to realize the emotional baggage that had weighed on my mind and body for a long time.

I hope this book will help you see that past-life regression is not just a spiritual practice but a powerful tool for mental, emotional, and physical healing. I invite you to join me on this journey to unravel your past and, in doing so, find the key to unlock a more peaceful and fulfilling present.

Through sharing my story, I want you to feel hope. I want you to realize that you are not alone in your struggles and that there is a path to healing that can help you live a happier life. My story is just the beginning—this book will guide you to find your way to healing, just as I did.

My Story

I was the only girl child among four siblings, and we were all happily married. My parents lived in Meerut while I was in Shillong with my family. I was very close to my father and my middle brother. In 1999, we lost my middle brother, Deepak, to cancer—a tremendous loss for all of us, but it hit my father the hardest.

Then, in 2008, everything changed. My father felt pain in his neck and shoulder while walking, and after a minor check-up, the doctor suggested a thorough heart check-up. My brothers Amar and Rajesh took him to Escorts Hospital in Delhi, where he was advised to undergo an angiography. The angiography revealed 80-90% blockages, and the doctors recommended an immediate bypass surgery. Without any hesitation, my brothers scheduled an immediate operation, and I was informed. I rushed to Delhi without a second thought. The surgery was done as scheduled.

When I met him after surgery in the observation room, he could recognize only me amongst all the family members and no one else. It was a huge shock for me. Being a Reiki healer, I started the healing process for his memory issues and an early recovery. To protect him from negative thoughts and energies, I didn't inform my family members about his memory loss. I was silently bearing the pain within. Later he was shifted to a private room and then after a few days was discharged and was asked to be back in the hospital for the opening of sutures after ten days.

Seven days later I left for my home town, Shillong to focus on my son's entrance exams for higher studies since he was just completing his board exams. I was in constant touch with my dad and kept healing him from a distance.

Another jolt came when it was found on his check-up that the doctors missed two stitches due to which he had severe pain in his legs and also his private parts were filled with water. Once again, he was admitted to the ICU in Delhi. Doctors diagnosed him with TB without waiting for the final report. It was later found that due to this wrong diagnosis and introduction of the medicine related to TB, his liver had been damaged. His condition started deteriorating and things started getting aggravated one after the other. We shifted him to the premier Sir Ganga Ram Hospital at Delhi for further treatment. In the meantime, he was having a bad bout of diarrhea due to the wrong medication given in the earlier hospital.

Once again, I rushed to Delhi and was informed that he needed a liver transplant, but this was not possible due to his old age and the major bypass surgery that he had just had. Now, it was just medicines and waiting and watching for him. I kept healing him throughout. Doctors told me that his time on earth was getting extended due to my healing.

Later from there, he was shifted to Anand Hospital in Meerut while continuing the medication prescribed from Delhi. However, there was not much improvement. It was hard to watch him deteriorate. I was trying to find a balance between my family life and Dad's health condition. Five months passed in and out of the hospital.

Then the day came. His vitals gradually dropped, and we lost him. I was there in the ICU, holding his hand as he left us. I became numb, my mind refusing to accept the cruel reality. How could he be gone?

A part of me was still waiting for him to walk into the room, smile at me, call my name—something to prove that this was just a terrible dream. But he didn't. And that silence was deafening. I stood frozen, the weight of loss numbing my body. The tears wouldn't come, even though I could feel them burning behind my eyes.

People around me begged me to release the grief, but I felt as if I had forgotten how to cry, slipping into depression. Nothing mattered to me anymore. Most days, I found myself retreating to the corner of my bed, knees pulled to my chest, staring at the blank walls. Words failed me, and even the sound of life around me felt distant, as though I had drifted away into a silent, cold world of my own.

When I lost him, it was as if the very foundation of my life had been ripped away. Once steady and full of his warmth, my world felt cold and hollow. The pain was overwhelming, like a heavy stone lodged in my chest, impossible to move, impossible to breathe around. Nothing could ever compare to the emptiness he left behind.

My husband, Rajiv, grew concerned and took me to a psychiatrist. I was put on medication and slept most of the day, yet nothing seemed to lift the weight of my sorrow. Rajiv decided to take me to Delhi for further treatment. I had lost a lot of weight; my appetite was gone.

Astral travel experience

Both of us left for the nearest airport at Guwahati to catch our flight to Delhi. Our flight was delayed and we were waiting for boarding. Suddenly, without any warning, I witnessed an out-of-body experience; this was the first time. I heard my dad's voice and felt I was moving toward higher realms escorted by him. I was able to hear all the sounds from below but was not able to see anyone.

During my astral travel in higher realms, I met all my deceased loved ones. I felt enveloped with their love. There was a warmth that filled my heart, and the happiness was pure. I was so happy and enjoying the new experience that I refused to return to my body.

My dad reminded me that my time on earth was not yet over, and that I needed to finish an unfinished task. His whispering voice was comforting, yet commanding. He also asked me to restart my daily meditation routine, which, in my grief, I had completely stopped after his demise. "Ask, and it shall be given to you", he said. Hearing this from him filled my eyes with tears.

I came back into the body and for the first time after his demise, felt comfortable and at peace with myself. It was as if my soul had been cradled in his love, and for the first time, I felt whole again, comfortable in the world he had left behind.

In Delhi, I was diagnosed as mentally sound and with no depression. That astral travel experience had brought me peace.

Encounter with past life.

I resumed practicing Meditation on a daily basis and during these meditation sessions, started getting messages from my dad and other spiritual masters. As I came out of these sessions, I would note down the messages in detail. Till today I have diaries full of those messages. One Sunday when I was meditating, I had a question in my mind: Why am I more connected with my dad than anyone else? My intention to get the reply transported me into the past life with my dad where I saw myself as his mother. He was my eldest son and closest to me in that life.

In this past life, I saw myself on my deathbed asking him to take care of his siblings when I was gone. This episode got me bewildered. I couldn't bear it and in utter disbelief, I fell from my chair where I had been sitting. But something deep within me told me it was true. This brought much solace to me. Rajiv was concerned and worried when

I told him about the revelation. A nonbeliever in such things, he said that I must be hallucinating since I was so attached to my dad. But I was already feeling better and more peaceful.

Now I started exploring past life regression through books and on the internet and came across **Dr. Newton Kondaveti** founder of *Life Research Academy* specializing in Past life regression and holistic healing therapies. I contacted him to understand better about my experiences, and doubts.

He helped me and assured me that I could trust the messages I receive from my dad in my meditation as he is my angel guide, taking me towards healing and altering the course of my life. I proceeded to take complete training in past life regression from Dr. Newton and Dr. Lakshmi.

Learning and Healing

Through past life regression methods, I uncovered many connections with my loved ones. My bond with my father, rooted in our past lives, brought deep insights. Integrating these lessons, I felt better and fully recovered from my depression.

I used Reiki to heal and balance my energy field, cleansing my aura and chakras daily. This routine freed me from negative thoughts and anxiety, allowing me to heal on every level—mentally, emotionally, physically and spiritually.

Day by day the messages I received changed my life and I found I was a changed person and spiritually more inclined. I started loving my new self. Now I was able to check on old thoughts and patterns surfacing in my mind and could easily work on them.

As I grew stronger, my healing practice evolved. I learnt more about mind-body healing, inner child healing, Kundalini healing, Colour therapy, water therapy, art therapy, and Neuro-Linguistic Programming (NLP). Each modality deepened my connection with myself and others. I became a practitioner, helping many people transform their lives.

A New Challenge

Just when I thought I had overcome the worst, a new challenge shook my world. Sometimes the Universe challenges us by throwing us harder challenges, completely uprooting all we have learnt so far. Following the earlier healing journey a new setback now came to face the family, and this was the hardest of all so far.

My daughter Dr. Rachita had got married in 2018 and was staying with her husband in Delhi after her final year of MD in Psychiatry and was waiting for her MD results. She was seven months pregnant and I was preparing to go for her delivery to Delhi which would have been in two months.

Suddenly the second wave of coronavirus spread dangerously in April 2021 in India, more severely in Delhi. While she was on maternity leave, her husband who had been attending his duties at the Hospital got the virus and she in turn contracted the virus from him. As she was not vaccinated due to pregnancy as per the protocols then being followed, she was badly affected.

Both were in Delhi managing by themselves and not

allowing us to visit to help them in fear that we may also get the virus during travel as we were also not fully vaccinated. My husband and I were worried and got ourselves vaccinated immediately, ready to leave for Delhi. She was weak. All through the day I was remotely healing her from Shillong.

But there was a big challenge in front of me; my 86-year-old mom staying with us at Shillong was suffering from Dementia and I had no help and was single-handedly looking after her. Mentally I was keeping myself strong by healing myself.

On the 16th April when she was recovering from corona, we got a call from my son-in-law that she was short of breath and her oxygen level was falling, and she needed urgent hospitalization. All the hospitals were full in Delhi.

Somehow, I managed to get her admitted to Sir Ganga Ram Hospital. Her treatment started and we left for Delhi immediately. On our way to catch our flight to Delhi , I spoke to her and she told me "Mom, I want to live. Please Save me." I didn't know then that those would be the last words I would ever hear from her.

Her last words, her voice was weak, barely more than a whisper over the phone, but her words hit me like a storm: 'Mom, I want to live.' Those five words shattered me. I wanted to reach through the miles between us and hold her, breathe life into her fragile body. But all I could do was stand there, helpless, as her voice faded away."

She was kept on a ventilator. She had already lost her unborn child the day she was admitted due to low oxygen levels.

I was given permission to visit the ICU in a PPE kit to give healing to her. Doctors told us her lungs had gone from bad to worse and despite all the best care and medication, we lost her on the 28th April 2021.

It felt as though the ground beneath me had crumbled, and I was left standing on the fragile shreds of my old world. My daughter had been my anchor, and now with her gone, I was adrift in an endless sea of sorrow. The weight of her absence was heavier than anything I had ever known. Once more I was back to square one with my mental state. It was too much for us to lose our child.

After her cremation, we immediately came back to Shillong as my mom was alone with my son. We were worried about them a lot. We were all dealing with our pains. I was healing everyone except myself to get released from pain. I got busy with household work and mom. My mind was not working and though I was working overtime I became very silent. I was consumed with guilt.

Then, just within 6 months, while we were still reeling under the impact of the corona virus, my mom decided to leave us for ever. After Rachita's departure, I had busied myself with the hectic care-giving routine that my mom's dementia required of me. Suddenly I was faced with the reality of the three deaths and nothing to do the whole day, except gloat over the past. I was left staring at a future which didn't exist as far as I was concerned and I slipped back into the worst bout of depression that I had ever had till date.

Healing Myself

I neglected myself while healing others, until one day, my husband reminded me of my strength as a healer. His words jolted me back to my healing. I began working on myself, erasing painful memories and the sounds of ambulances in my head through NLP.

I later explored my past life with my daughter, and she revealed that she had chosen, by her free will, to leave. Her body could no longer bear the trauma, and she didn't want to live a burdened life. She gave me the strength to move forward and finish my mission of spreading the power of healing.

Revelation

I realized that healing is not a one-time process but an ongoing journey to be followed to graduate and remain updated in the journey of life; in progressing in all the fields mentally, emotionally, physically, and spiritually. I had added to my repertoire many more methods of healing than I had earlier such as mind-body healing, Inner child healing, Kundalini healing, Colour Therapy, Water therapy, Art therapy and Neuro-linguistic programming by learning them professionally.

I felt that if I could help heal and be useful to others, it would not only lessen my pain but I would also be self-healing. Once I learnt the methods I started helping others by healing them and bringing profound change in their lives.

My Mission in life is to bring change in people's lives worldwide by making them understand the power of healing and inspiring them to adopt healing in everyday life. We want more healers in the present time when we are going through so much of a crisis in the area of mental, physical, emotional and spiritual health.

The purpose of sharing my story is to inspire you and help you understand the profound impact of healing. In the following chapters, I will explain past life regression and offer self-help techniques that will empower you to heal yourself. Healing is freedom, and once you experience it, you will find peace.

Affirmations one can practice in daily life –

"I am open to healing all parts of myself, past and present."

"I release the weight of past traumas and step into my true power." "I trust in my ability to heal and transform my life."

"I am worthy of love, joy, and peace in this lifetime."

"My journey of healing is leading me toward greater self-awareness and fulfillment."

"The wound is the place where the light enters you."
- Rumi

2. COMMON MYTHS/MISCONCEPTIONS

"Our wounds are often the openings into the best and most beautiful part of us."
- David Richo

In this chapter, you will discover that many of the myths and misconceptions we carry about healing are simply untrue. We often hear things from people, read about them, or encounter experiences online. Unfortunately, not everyone provides the complete picture. And as we all know; half-knowledge can be dangerous.

Healing, whether through Past life regression, Reiki, or other techniques, often faces doubts, fears, and questions about authenticity. Here, we'll explore these challenges and offer solutions to overcome the mental blocks that prevent people from embracing healing practices. Understanding and addressing these challenges is the first step towards achieving a balanced and healthy life—physically, mentally, emotionally, and spiritually.

Once your doubts clear, you will find the breakthrough you've been waiting for. We'll focus specifically on past life regression and Reiki healing to help you overcome your fears.

Whenever I am conducting a workshop in past life regression people always have a question before enrolling for the session about the authenticity of it all.

I know it must be working in your mind too. It's not fully accepted like other conventional methods of medicine. However, this is widely practiced by practitioners to heal people through it. The theory is based on incarnation which is still not believed in all religions. Many known psychiatrists and mental health doctors have applied it to their patients all over the world.

Dr. Brian Weiss is one important name amongst those who applied it to their patients facing problems in their present lives. When his patient was treated through hypnosis and slipped into a past life it was a revelation to him. Later he documented the sessions conducted in series in his book- *"Many Lives Many Masters"* one of the books that gives great insight into the many lives one has lived in the past.

Many doctors worked tirelessly with their patients and explored their past lives between lives. *"Journey of Souls"* is another book by **Dr. Michael Newton** who documented the cases of his patients of life-between-life stages in this book.

My goal is to offer you sufficient understanding and

real-life case histories, opening the door to acceptance. Once you begin to embrace this knowledge without fear or doubt, you'll realize these techniques are safe and effective—regardless of your prior beliefs. Wholeheartedly accepting them will invite a positive transformation toward well-being.

Let's explore some of the most common myths and misconceptions in various healing modalities.

Myth and misconception about Past Life Regression

#Fear: The very first myth is-what if I get stuck in a past life and am not able to come back.

This is just a fear in your mind. One common fear that holds people back from exploring this practice is the idea of getting stuck in a past life during a session.

Solution- These techniques are done under trained practitioners and even if practising on oneself, one should be well trained to conduct a self-session. One remains in control and remembers everything he or she visualizes in bits and pieces.

This is just like a guided meditation in which you completely silence your conscious mind to explore the memories surfacing from the past. With the insight of a complete session, you can find the connection of these past memories with present issues that you are suffering.

#Misconception: Past life regression is just making stories in the mind as it's not true.

Why didn't the mind make some other story?

#Doubting authenticity: People also think it's baseless and not true and fooling people. They doubt the authenticity.

Many books written by experts like **Dr. Brian Weiss** and **Michael Newton** document countless past life experiences, lending credibility to this practice.

#Myth: Some people think they will be able to see the full story of their past life.

Truth --

They only see the past life in fragments and by connecting these with the present life habits, patterns, traumas and pain you get insight.

#Fear: Some people also think if past life memories are not good, they will be traumatized by reliving the trauma. Past life trauma will open wounds in the present life and will be overwhelming and so hesitate to go for it.

Solution –

When you visualize past life trauma with detachment, resolution takes place by understanding the emotional connections with the present life. If ever one feels challenged emotionally during a session the practitioner helps you to come out from those emotions.

One always remains in control. Once the revelation takes place, your anxiety, pain and depression disappear. One feels lighter and free from the baggage carried for so long in fear of losing authenticity. Till now you were scared to work on the issues and you became habituated to living with them as a part of your life.

#Fear: Past life regression will hamper their religion and beliefs.

Solution– Remember that as a soul, you have lived many lives across different religions.

Let me share a case that might ease your mind.

A woman in her late forties visited for a session with the problem she was facing in her workplace with subordinates and colleagues. She mentioned she had been recently posted in the city and no one liked her in her office and she could sense their dislike for her to the point that she felt they hated her. While they had no option but to respect her command as she was their senior, but they did so without any sense of belonging. She tried many times to get closer to them but found them cold and remote.

When regressed into past life she witnessed herself as a leader of a religious sect, in which due to the wrong learning and guidance from religious masters she massacred many people in the name of religion.

She could connect that these were the same people now working presently in her office. When taken into another life in the same session she saw herself as a priest in church reading the Bible.

In another life, she saw herself in a Hindu family. After the process of forgiveness, she was brought back to the present. She was crying loudly and asking everyone present there- Who am I? What's my religion. I was Muslim,

Christian and Hindu in different lives. This reveals that the soul has no religion. We usually follow the religion of the family we are born in. This insight brought in a lot of change in her and by integrating the same, her relationship with others in the workplace became better. Besides, she was also now more inclined towards spirituality.

I hope this helped you to understand better, and respect all religions which ultimately teach the same lessons.

#Misconception: There is also a misconception that we come back to the present life with the same set of people as in the past- life.

This is not true; the soul only comes back with other souls with whom they have to settle some karma, or they come to help the other soul learn their life lessons and teachings.

#Present life traumas: There is another question – how will we find out from which past life we are facing the particular problem in the present life?

Solution – the trained therapist or practitioner very well knows how to connect the previous life with the problem of present life through 'intentions'.

Let's explore more myths of different modalities that can help you to understand better which compliment each other.

"Common Myths About Reiki", "How Reiki Works" Reiki Healing

Reiki, an ancient Japanese healing practice, was founded by **Dr. Mikao Usui**. It is widely regarded as a powerful alternative therapy, embraced by people around the world for its ability to restore balance and promote healing. Despite its popularity, many misconceptions surround Reiki, and in this chapter, we will address these fears and doubts, offering clarity to those seeking its benefits.

#Myth: A widespread myth is that Reiki is a religious practice, which may interfere with one's own beliefs.

This is entirely false. Reiki is pure universal energy, completely detached from any religion. Like the elements—wind, heat, or cold—the energy itself carries no religious identity.

#Myth: People spiritually inclined, and full of intuition can only practice reiki.

This big myth has created a huge confusion in society. Perhaps spread by people who tried to practice it, when it didn't work for them. This could have happened since they may not have learnt the practice from a trained teacher or didn't understand the method correctly and applied it wrongly which created this myth.

Anyone who learns from a trained therapist will be able to practice it and can heal themselves and others. In the first degree of reiki, you can heal by touch but the best part is that in the second degree you can send the reiki healing from a distance by connecting to your clients sitting in another place, city or country. This way anyone can access healing from anyone located in any part of the world.

One can manifest any goal. Addictions can be cured only by opening the blocked energy to allow free flow in the chakras. One can connect with a higher self to get insight and manifest whatever one wants as their intuition becomes stronger.

#Myth: Reiki will not work on a person who is not open about healing.

It will work on anyone whether they believe, accept, or not.

#Fear: Reiki healing disturbs energy levels, which many people fear.

Solution: Reiki is practiced to clean any blockages from your aura as well as chakras through energy healing for good health and achieving your goals. One feels more energetic, vibrant, and full of insight by being able to manage life on all levels. Millions of people are taking advantage of reiki, and have decided to make it the way of living.

#Concern: We lose energy, and sending reiki to others makes us weak.

When practising Reiki, one is driving energy from the universe and becomes a channel to transfer energy to the person who needs healing. When you are receiving energy from the universe, some part of the energy is absorbed by your body to heal you and strengthen you on all levels. One never feels, weak and drained by healing others.

Physical and mental healing through Psychic Surgery

This is practiced by reiki healers, as well as independently by those who have learnt this technique.

This is widely practiced for healing on an energy level connecting with clients' minds to heal them. In this, the intention is first set to heal and then connected by different methods. Profound healing takes place most of the time in one session but sometimes few sessions are required, based on complexity.

You can heal clients from a distance or nearby. It is a non-invasive process, where the healer works on the energy level. No touch is required in this healing with the client's body. There is no opening or cutting of the body and no loss of blood takes place. The whole session is performed in a meditative state connecting with the mind.

This also can be practiced with other conventional medical treatments without interfering with them. There is no harm created by performing psychic healing through psychic surgery.

Healing through Psychic Surgery

Here's a case history of a client in his thirties. His mother came to me and asked for help through healing for her son in Delhi. He had suffered from acute pain in his lower abdomen and had gone for a checkup to the doctor.

When the reports came in, it was found that one of the kidneys was displaced from its place due to which urgent surgery was required. I asked her to give me a week to heal him completely. He deferred the date of surgery giving an excuse to his doctor that he was not getting leave from his office and so borrowed some time. The doctor given him medicine to manage the pain for this period and he was asked to take rest.

I told his mother that I would perform surgery the next morning. He lay down as directed by me in a quiet place as I performed psychic surgery on him. He later told me that while the surgery was going on, he could feel that something was moving inside him in the kidney area.

After the Psychic surgery, his pain disappeared completely. I gave him two more sessions to heal completely and to accept the changes made within a week. After a week I asked him to go to the doctor and get sonography done once again. He followed my instructions. When the doctor saw the report he couldn't believe it and said, I am surprised how come it's back in its original place without any surgery? This is a more than fifteen years old case, and it has never relapsed. He is hale and hearty, living a healthy life.

He sent me his testimonial, where he mentioned his miraculous healing which saved him from conventional surgery. He was so very grateful and happy, regaining full health.

#Concern: Also understood as a hoax, as some practitioners fake it.

If the session is done under a trained practitioner, it certainly works. Many people benefit from this; I myself practice this technique in healing myself and others, with miraculous results.

#Interference: Also misunderstood, this hampers conventional surgery and will hurt them.

Clients are never asked to stop conventional surgery as this can be performed along with conventional surgery without any hindrance for best results.

#Misconception: It's also mistaken that it's meant only for serious patients.

It's again a myth- one can apply this healing to both simple and serious illnesses.

Psychic surgery remains one of my favourite healing techniques because of its speed and effectiveness. The results are often immediate and long-lasting, making it a powerful tool in the realm of energy healing.

Practicing Meditation for Focus

Before going for past regression, learning meditation helps to focus the mind.

Myths surrounding meditation:

#Concern: It's difficult to sit in one place, and focus without any thought for a long time.

Maybe you are misguided or misinformed by people or picked up the knowledge from somewhere. Just imagine, if you could empty a room of its air. Not possible, right? as fresh air will replace that vacuum. In the same way, our thoughts keep coming and going. Just be a spectator to those thoughts with detachment. Gradually, the thoughts will slow down and calmness will prevail.

Some people say that whenever they sit to meditate, all their unfinished tasks rush to the forefront. In this case, starting with guided meditation can help keep the mind occupied, and prevent it from wandering—especially when you're mentally busy or disturbed.

Breath meditation

Breath meditation can also seem challenging when trying to focus for longer than a minute. It's normal for the mind to wander; the practice lies in bringing your focus back. While it may feel difficult at first, with practice, even five minutes of concentration is a victory.

Inner child healing

This is the most powerful technique used for childhood traumas, faced by all of us.

Myth: One thinks, that by opening their childhood wounds they will feel vulnerable Attending to wounds from childhood, and releasing them brings more strength and clarity within.

In conventional techniques like CBT and DBT, this is used by psychiatrists worldwide.

Fear: If touched, childhood wounds will manifest blockages in the present.

While addressing these issues, the transformation takes place by releasing the painful memories from childhood. When you see from the lens of an adult with understanding, you can forgive yourself and others for whatever happened in their childhood.

One releases fear, anxiety and guilt, carried for so long, and resolves the issue of freedom.

Mind-Body Healing technique

Mind-body healing is a technique pioneered by **Brandon Bays**, who successfully healed herself from a football-sized tumor in her stomach. She shares her incredible journey in her book, *The Journey*, where she details methods for both physical and emotional healing. You can read her book or learn these techniques from her directly, or through her trained practitioners.

This healing method focuses on addressing and releasing bad memories stored in the body, whether from the present or past lives, to restore balanced health on all levels.

Doubt: "How can memories manifest disease in the mind and body?"

This is a common question asked by skeptical clients. Scientifically, it has been proven that our thoughts can manifest as physical ailments in the body. These thoughts can lead to conditions like anxiety, stress, depression, and physical diseases such as cancer, migraines, autoimmune disorders, and chronic pain.

Many times, doctors are unable to identify the source of these pains, or provide long-term cures. This happens because negative experiences, when left unresolved, become stored in our cells, and over time, they can manifest as physical illnesses in the corresponding areas of the body.

Healing through Mind-body healing:

Here I am sharing my self-healing with this technique.

I started feeling pain in my right heel, and gradually the pain increased over a period of time. Now, it needed attention, hampering my walk. I was diagnosed with Plantar fasciitis, a condition that causes inflammation of the plantar fascia, a thick band of tissue that runs from the heel to the toes and forms the arch of the foot. Symptoms include acute pain and stiffness, aching or burning in the bottom of the foot. It gets intense in the morning when you get up. I was asked to do some specific exercises and wear special shoes and sandals meant for this problem. I was also told to accept that I'd have to live with the pain for the rest of my life.

That was when I decided to explore mind-body healing for myself.

Exploration:

While exploring, and as memories surfaced, I found there was a guilt that I suffered from- of not being able to breastfeed my child due to septic in my sutures after delivery. This led to my child having a weaker immune system, and for two decades, I unknowingly held onto that guilt.

Revelation:

This was an old memory of twenty years back and was

settled in my right heel which manifested this pain. After releasing this memory, with self-forgiveness, my pain disappeared within a single night. The next morning, when I got up there was no pain, and I felt on top of the world. It's already been more than ten years since and the pain has never returned.

Neuro Linguistic Programming

NLP was developed by **Richard Bandler** and **John Grinder**, who believed that the thought patterns and behaviors of successful individuals could be identified and taught to others. NLP therapists use various techniques, such as reframing negative thoughts, anchoring positive emotions, and teaching effective communication skills, to help individuals achieve their desired outcomes.

Some people, due to a lack of understanding, are hesitant to try NLP. It has been labeled as pseudoscience.

Fears: Practitioners might manipulate or influence people.

However, this technique is designed to help individuals alter the wrong and unhelpful habits and patterns, and replace them with useful ones that work for you by changing the submodalities (the specific qualities of a person's internal representation of an experience or sensation. They are the subsets of the five modalities, or senses, that people use to process information.) of thought patterns already present in one's mind. Though not always scientifically validated, NLP delivers quick and impactful results, especially in areas of personal growth and well-being.

Though it is not supported scientifically, this brings

therapeutic effects, in a short period and is widely practiced by practitioners worldwide. One can bring change in one's patterns and habits through this technique. I practice this in everyday life and to help others, to bring change in habits and patterns with transformative results.

Belief: Considered by some as pseudoscience and dismissed. They think it's only about positive thinking.

Though not proven scientifically, this technique brings everlasting change in people. Results speak for themselves and hence this method is very popular amongst healers.

Misconception: One needs to be an expert, to benefit from NLP.

NLP techniques are simple and after learning can be self-applied, making it accessible for personal development. It's a tool that makes life easier. NLP is flexible and can be tailored to suit different people as per their needs which makes it effective for a wide range of people, whether one believes in it or not.

All the techniques I have explained are meant to bring healing and growth into your life. I practice them myself, so I can personally vouch for their effectiveness. It's important to note that you don't have to use every single technique— just choose the ones you feel most comfortable with. You can also learn from trained practitioners, or apply the methods mentioned in this book.

Consistency is key. These techniques should be used continuously, not just once, to truly see transformation and growth. Healing is an ongoing process that prepares us for the challenges in life.

I hope this chapter has helped clear some of your myths and misconceptions, offering a broader understanding of how you can embrace these methods to bring balance and wellness into your life. By overcoming these myths and misconceptions you are opening a door for healing and self-discovery.

Intentions for the release of all myths and misconceptions:

"I release all fears and misconceptions about healing practices and open myself to new possibilities."

"I trust in the healing process and know that I am always safe and supported."

"I embrace the truth that healing is available to everyone, including myself."

"I am open to exploring new healing methods without judgment."

"I allow myself to experience the full depth of healing in whatever form it takes."

The next chapter will explore how to address the specific problems and fears that may be stopping you from achieving your goals and how to start applying the healing techniques that can transform your life towards freedom and a fulfilled life. The major key is, that healing is available for everyone and anyone can practice it by learning these techniques.

Call to Action

What myths and misconceptions do you carry about past life regression?

____

____

What Myths and misconceptions do you carry about Reiki?

____

____

Are you able to focus during meditation? What distracts you?

____

____

Have you ever tried inner child healing? Do you think it could help you?

____

____

What's your understanding of psychic surgery?

____

____

Have you ever explored alternative healing? If yes, which ones?

____

____

"The greatest discovery of any generation is that a human being can alter his life by altering his attitude."
- William James

3. INITIAL HICCUPS AND HURDLES

"Healing is a matter of time, but it is sometimes also a matter of opportunity."
- Hippocrates.

In this chapter, we'll delve into the initial challenges and obstacles that one may encounter when embarking on a transformative journey.

Healing is not always a smooth path. It often comes with its share of hurdles. When we begin the process of transformation, no matter which healing technique we choose, it requires a great deal of patience, perseverance, and faith.

Each challenge that arises is a stepping stone, guiding us toward a healthier, more fulfilling life. You might find yourself wondering as to which healing method to start with, as I've introduced several in the earlier chapters. Don't feel overwhelmed by the choices—begin with one.

Start with something simple, like meditation. Guided meditation is a wonderful way to focus your mind, and once you feel comfortable with it, you can explore other practices like past life regression. This powerful technique allows you to connect your past experiences to your present life, helping you understand where certain challenges originate.

The insights you gain will shift your perspective, and with time and practice, positive changes will begin to manifest. Afterward, you can explore Reiki or any other healing practice that resonates with you.

Facing the Hiccups and Hurdles

As you embark on this healing journey, you may encounter various obstacles. Let's address a few of the common fears and misconceptions.

Fear of Painful Emotions Surfacing

Don't get scared by the idea that buried emotions, surfacing during sessions of past life regression, will create a lot of painful emotional feelings.

This will not create any emotional turbulence, as the practitioner will guide you with utmost care. You'll learn to observe these emotions with detachment, almost like watching a movie, which helps prevent any emotional overwhelm.

If you do happen to feel connected to those emotions, your practitioner will help you navigate through them safely. Understanding that these events occurred in a past life brings clarity and peace.

Unpleasant Sensations in the Body

This fear could perplex you and restrain you from going in for a session. Someone, having gone through past life regression may have told you this, but perhaps did not furnish sufficient clarity, which prevents you from sailing in the ship of healing.

Any sensations where you feel pain, restlessness or emotions are a sign that transformation is taking place. One needs to allow oneself confidence to release all the pains and traumas for complete healing. To ensure healing, one must not freeze or block the pain and memories.

The Fear of Fabricated Memories

Some may wonder if the stories uncovered during past life regression are just fabricated by the mind. If that were the case, why would the mind create these particular memories and not some others? The memories that arise are stored in your subconscious, linked to past experiences.

A fascinating case study sheds light on this:

Mother and daughter, both came for their session for past life regression, and they both were sent to different practitioners in different rooms to explore the past life at the same time. They did not have any contact during the session.

When they both finished and met and shared in the presence of a practitioner, they were amazed to find they both reached the same past life in which they were husband and wife. This case study opens the door to understanding that stories are not fabricated by the mind. Many such types of cases are documented as eye-openers.

Incidents such as these, well-documented and verified, help us understand that the mind isn't fabricating these experiences—these memories are a reflection of past lives stored in the subconscious.

Unrealistic Expectations of Quick Healing

Don't keep any unrealistic expectations from your session. Sometimes, you need more than one session as per the requirement of your problem. Healing is an ongoing process, and healing takes its time. An unrealistic expectation will lead you towards frustration. Enjoy and celebrate small positive changes as you claim small victories.

Breaking Free from Habits and Patterns

If you are habituated to avoiding challenging situations and remain stuck in the same habits and patterns, you will never move forward. But once you make a decision, and take action, you will be freed from these debilitating habits.

Consistency is the mantra to achieve desired goals. So don't be reluctant; take steps towards your freedom. Healing is not a destination, but a journey. Each small success is worth celebrating, and every obstacle you overcome brings you closer to a life of freedom, balance, and fulfilment. Trust the process, stay consistent, and know that you have the strength to heal and grow.

Relapses: Embracing Setbacks on Your Healing Journey

When relapses take place, you may start losing trust in the process, thinking it's just a temporary fix. Whatever is resurfacing needs more opportunity for deeper growth and healing. Setbacks are a normal part of healing, like any other conventional field. Once again, I remind you that healing is an ongoing process, and one has all the power to fix it.

The initial hiccups and hurdles at the beginning of the healing journey are temporary and manageable. You can fix them with the right mindset, and with the tools given in this book.

Understanding each obstacle is an opportunity to get stronger, and more resilient. By addressing these common difficulties and staying committed to the process, you can easily and successfully achieve the early stage of healing and prepare yourself for lasting transformation.

Trust the journey

Be patient with yourself, and embrace the small victories on the way. Don't get bothered by those who judge you. It's your life, so take the command in your hand. It's your journey of growth.

Once people find positive changes in you, you would start getting their support and they too could be attracted toward a healing journey of their own. Be a role model for others by practicing these methods in your life.

Past Life Regression: Self-Practice Through Meditation

The easiest way is to explore past life is by recording in your own voice, the script given in this book. While listening to the script with a relaxed mind and body, choose a silent place where you can easily explore past life memories.

But if you opt for healing via trained professionals, profound healing and integration will take place, as you will be getting trained insight and will understand different aspects connected with your present life. You will quickly witness growth in different areas of your life.

Triggers that we face in present life have deep-rooted causes and are connected with past life. Once you start healing, the results will surely make you feel like a champion, living a healthy and peaceful life, free from stress and anxiety. You will be calm in your approach and will be focused on different areas of life without any difficulties.

You will deal with problems like a pro. You will advocate to others the benefit of healing, and inspire them to embrace it in their lives. The sense of fulfillment and achievement will bring lots of confidence. You will be prepared for more challenges in life and deal with them easily. People will listen to your advice and will follow you.

Journaling Your Hiccups and Hurdles

Writing down your fears, challenges, and experiences can provide clarity. Use the following questions to help guide your journaling process:

Are you scared of taking past life regression sessions? What are your major fears, and why? List them.

____

____

____

What emotional resistance do you face whenever you plan to go for a session, and why?

____

____

____

Do you have unrealistic expectations from past life regression? Write them down.

____

____

____

Do you face trust issues regarding past life regression therapy? Summarize your thoughts in a few words.

____

____

____

Affirmations to Practice

Before going for a session, use these affirmations to help you deal with any hiccups or hurdles:

"I am patient with myself as I heal, knowing that every step I take is part of my journey."

"I trust in the process of healing and embrace the challenges that arise as opportunities for growth."

"I release fear and resistance, welcoming the lessons and insights from my past with an open heart."

"I honor my emotions and allow them to surface, knowing they are guiding me toward deeper healing."

"I am supported by the universe and those around me as I courageously face my past and heal."

Remember,

"Healing takes courage, and we all have courage, even if we have to dig a little to find it."
- Tori Amos.

Embrace your healing journey with trust, courage, and resilience. Every step, no matter how small, is leading you toward a healthier, happier life.

4. THE SOLUTION/PROCESS

"The only way to heal is to go through the wound, not around it."
- Unknown.

In this chapter, we will walk through the systematic process of healing, using Past Life Regression as the foundation, along with complementary techniques like meditation and Reiki.

Meditation is used to calm our conscious mind and explore the subconscious mind. Let's see the technique of meditation. Meditation will be used further for past life regression techniques.

Set aside 10 to 15 minutes daily for meditation, focusing on mindfulness and self-reflection. Choose a silent place, sit in a comfortable position, and close your eyes. Take a deep breath - three to four times. Start watching your thoughts with detachment, like you watch a movie and don't get attached to them.

If you get attached, your emotions will overwhelm you. Initially, you will find thoughts are flooding in, but gradually they will slow down, and the mind will start getting calm. While reflecting on your thoughts your stress and anxiety will diminish.

Use guided meditation, specially designed for past life regression for progressive relaxation. Or you can choose one of the many kinds of guided meditations from YouTube. Here in this meditation, you will go deep within and explore, but do not follow the steps to enter the past life initially, in order not to get confused. Practice guided meditation daily and feel the healing within. Meditation prepares the mind for deep introspection.

Guided Meditation Technique

This is a technique I developed for myself. If you find it comfortable and suitable, feel free to use it.

Steps to follow –

Sit in a quiet place, and take a comfortable position. Close your eyes.

Start relaxing your body, from toe to head by tightening and relaxing each part.

Now bring your focus in between your eyebrows, in the third eye area.

Visualize a white light in the third eye area in the form of a ball.

Now see - that the ball of white light is moving clockwise. First slowly, and then getting faster. This is your soul.

Now, see this soul in the form of white light, coming out from the third eye (area between eyebrows) and standing in front of you.

You, the soul, can watch your physical body sitting still, in front of you.

If you are sitting in some closed place, see yourself coming out from the ceiling of the room and rising above, without any effort. If in an open place, then also keep rising above.

Keep moving higher and higher, and feel yourself amongst the clouds. Enjoy being there, and again keep rising.

Now you will find the moon, in front of you. Just greet the moon (good morning or evening, depending on whatever time you are undertaking this journey). You can talk to the moon, say whatever you feel like and if there is any message the moon wants to convey, listen with gratitude, say bye, and move higher.

Now, you are facing the sun. It's so bright, you can feel the warmth and even touch the sun as the soul has no body and doesn't get burnt.

Now talk to the sun, and listen if there is any message for you. Once again say bye and move higher.

Now, you are in front of a big gate. Open the gate, and enter inside.

There is a beautiful river, flowing in front of you. Trees on the side, are laden with fruits and flowers.

Where you are standing, there are two paths, one going right and the other to the left.

Take the path to your left, and walk along the river. There is a tunnel in front of you. Enter the tunnel and keep moving until it's dark, but don't get scared and keep moving straight. Now you can see a faint light coming from the end of the tunnel in the direction you are moving.

Gradually, this light is becoming brighter and brighter, and you find the end of the tunnel.

Come out of the tunnel, and keep moving in the direction of the light. This light is guiding you. Now, you are closer to the light, in the form of a big divine ball.

There is a flat ground in front of that bright light. Sit down on the ground. Spend some time here, and if you have any questions in your mind, ask within.

You will see, after some time, there will be an answer to the question within your mind. (Trust the answer, as it's coming from your divine self. If the answer is not coming, never mind, as you will hear the answer later after meditation from someone, or on TV or you will read it somewhere.)

This is optional if you feel like asking a question, otherwise, after some time you get up and take the journey back.

You can walk back through the tunnel and path, come out from the gate, and take a journey downwards. You will find the sun and moon on the way, as well. You will, once again enter in the clouds and gradually into your room, from the ceiling and will come down in front of your body. Now, slowly enter back through your third eye.

Take some time, and whenever you are ready, rub your palms, put them on your eyes, and then slowly remove them and open your eyes.

Feel the relaxation in mind and body.

You can record the above process in your voice slowly, and listen to the recording while doing the above meditation.

Other Types of Meditation

Mindfulness Meditation: Stay present in the moment, feeling body sensations while meditating.

Breath Meditation: Focus on your breath as it moves in and out through your nose.

Chakra Meditation: Focus on your chakras, sending energy to each one. Balance all seven chakras to align your physical, emotional, mental and spiritual states.

All these meditation techniques can be practiced in conjunction with past life regression and Reiki healing.

Understanding Past Life Regression

Past life regression is the practice of exploring one's past life through progressive relaxation, which one can attain through meditation or hypnosis, done by a trained practitioner to uncover the root cause of trauma, pains, emotional blocks, or recurring patterns.

Past life regression helps to release these negative influences in the individual's life, to bring healing and personal growth. Unresolved traumas or emotional baggage from past lives can manifest in the present as phobias, fears, physical illness or emotionally disturbing patterns. By gaining clarity on these issues, healing can take place.

Past life regression typically involves guided meditation, where the individual is led into a relaxed state. From this state, memories of past life may surface, which gives insight into the present.

Actions to Take

Here are some key actions to begin your journey of healing:

1. **Find a Qualified Practitioner:** For the best results, start by working with a trained professional in past life regression.

2. **Reflect on Memories and Emotions:** The emotions and memories that surface during your session hold the key to your healing and transformation.
3. **Integrate Insights:** Apply the wisdom you gain during your sessions to your current life, releasing patterns that no longer serve you.

Reiki complements past life regression.

Past life regression helps individuals to release emotional traumas, pain, and patterns from past lives; in the same way Reiki brings healing on a cellular and energy level. One can bring harmony and balance into life by integrating emotions and insights gained from past life regression.

For this, the individual needs to learn Reiki from trained practitioners for initiation, and understanding of the technique. Practicing mindfulness every day brings healing, by allowing healing energy to work effectively. Individuals can also get help from practitioners.

How NLP compliments past life regression

NLP techniques consist of reframing, anchoring positive emotions, and practicing new ways of thinking to get rid of old patterns in individuals. This practice, combined with meditation and Reiki, can help you create new pathways for healing and growth.

The power of self-healing

Healing is a self-driven process. Techniques given are tools that one can use to facilitate one's own healing. The real transformation however, comes from within.

Don't wait to take the first step.

Daily Affirmations: Before starting meditation, repeat these affirmations to center yourself. Choose the one that resonates most with you:

"With every breath, I let go of old patterns and make space for renewal and growth."

"I release past traumas and welcome the light of healing into every part of my being."

"My body, mind, and soul are aligned and work together for my highest good."

"I trust the process of healing, knowing that each step leads me closer to inner peace."

Practicing meditation every day for five to ten minutes is the first step, and over time, you can gradually extend the duration as it becomes a natural part of your routine. It's best to start with guided meditation, as it helps you maintain focus and prevents you from feeling overwhelmed or losing interest, especially when trying other, more challenging forms of meditation.

As you meditate, make it a habit to journal your experiences. Take note of the sensations and emotions that arise in both your mind and body. These reflections can be powerful in tracking your progress and understanding any insights or answers that come to you during your practice.

Before diving into past life regression, it's essential to first undergo womb regression, to explore memories from the early stages of the present life and begin healing from there.

WOMB REGRESSION/ AGE REGRESSION

You can begin the process using any induction technique, but I love progressive relaxation. In the next chapter, I've outlined the progressive relaxation technique that I have used for past life regression. You can follow it up until the person reaches their favourite place and then continue with the instructions below.

Now, I will count from 5 to 1, and as I do so, allow yourself to return to any significant moment from the last year. It could be a pleasant or unpleasant memory from your birthday, wedding anniversary, or any other day that holds meaning for you.

Five... Go back to any significant moment from last year.
Four... Try to recall the details of the memory.
Three... Focus on the memories, sensations, and feelings that arise.
Two... Relive the experience as if it's happening right now.
One... Feel all the emotions and sensations in your body at this moment. Be fully present and relive the memory.

Now, take a moment to look around.

What are you doing?

What are you experiencing?

Is anyone with you, or are you alone?

Is it day or night?

Are you indoors or outside?

What is the significance of this memory?

If the memory is happy, allow yourself to relive it. Let that happiness flood your entire body, filling you with warmth.

If the memory is unpleasant, I want you to fully experience those painful feelings as if they are happening now. Allow these emotions to intensify, but only to a level where you can still bear them.

(It's okay if you feel like crying—it's a release, a catharsis taking place.)

Now, feel all these emotions in your body. Where exactly are you feeling them? Describe the sensations happening within.

Is it a heavy or light feeling?

What colour and shape would you give these sensations?

Now, change that colour and shape into something vibrant that makes you feel positive and at ease.

Since this memory has now been brought to your awareness, it's beginning to lose its hold over you. You are feeling lighter, and free.

At this moment, detach yourself from the memory. Imagine

floating above the scene, observing it from a distance.

Now, I will count again from 5 to 1. This time, you will go back to any significant moment from your college days. You are going to relive and re-experience those moments.

Five... Go back to a significant moment from your college years.
Four... Remember and recall the details of the memory.
Three... Focus on the sensations and impressions that arise in your body. What images come to mind?
Two... Relive the experience as if it's happening now.
One... Feel the flood of emotions.

Be fully present in this memory and let it unfold before you.

If the memory is unpleasant, I want you to fully experience those painful feelings as if they are happening now. Allow these emotions to intensify, but only to a level where you can still bear them.

(It's okay if you feel like crying—it's a release, a catharsis taking place.)

Now, feel all these emotions in your body.

Where exactly are you feeling them?

Describe the sensations happening within. Is it a heavy or light feeling?

What color and shape would you give these sensations?

Now, change that color and shape into something vibrant,

something that makes you feel positive and at ease.

Since this memory has now been brought to your awareness, it's beginning to lose its hold over you. You are feeling lighter, and free.

At this moment, detach yourself from the memory. Imagine floating above the scene, observing it from a distance.

Now, I will count from 1 to 5. This time, go back to a significant moment from your school years.

Five... Return to a significant memory from school.
Four... Recall the details and relive them.
Three... Focus on the impressions, feelings, and sensations you are experiencing now.
Two... Relive this memory as though it's happening in the present moment.
One... Feel all the emotions.

Be in the memory. Look at the details of your school, the building, your teachers, your favourite games, friends, and the feelings you had back then. How do you feel about them now?

If the memory is unpleasant, feel it to the extent that you can handle it. Notice where in your body you feel it, and again, change the color and shape into something positive.

As these memories come back to you, they begin to lose their power. You are feeling lighter, and more at peace.

Detach yourself from this moment and float above the scene.

Now, as I count from 5 to 1, go back to a significant moment when you were in your mother's womb.

Five... Going back to a significant moment in the womb.
Four... Recall the details of this memory.
Three... Focus on the sensations, feelings, images, and impressions that arise.
Two... Relive the experience as if it's happening now.
One... Feel all the emotions.

Be there, fully immersed in the memory.

How do you feel inside the womb?

Is it tight or spacious?

Is it dark or is there some light?

Do you feel warm or cold?

What is your mother doing?

Can you feel your parents' emotions toward you?

Are they happy?

Now, I am going to count from 1 to 5. As I count, you will relieve your birth memory—the moment you entered this world.

One... Trust the feelings, sensations, and impressions that arise.

Two... Feel everything happening in your body as you come through the birth canal.
Three... Do you feel eager to come out, or are you scared?
Four... Who is present as you are born?
Five... Do you feel welcomed by your parents, grandparents, and family?

Relive the entire birth experience. Trust the impressions that arise.

Is the memory pleasant or traumatic? If it's unpleasant, allow yourself to feel it fully, letting the emotions intensify to a bearable level.

Now, focus on where in your body you are feeling this memory. Describe the sensations.

Are they overwhelming or light? If they are overwhelming, notice the colour and shape. Change it into a colour and shape that represents positive emotions.

As this memory comes into your consciousness, it begins to lose its power. You are free from its hold.

Detach yourself from the moment and float above the scene.

Now, I will count from 1 to 3, and with each count, you will return to the present moment, feeling refreshed and rejuvenated.

One... Start moving your body gently.
Two... Feel awake and revitalized in the present moment.
Three... Be happy that you have completed your womb/age regression.

You may omit the final three steps to return to the present, or, if you wish, you can explore past lives. You can also return to the present and schedule a past life session for a later time.

I prefer to do these regressions in two sittings for better results. Don't forget to heal and integrate any trauma or unpleasant memories from the womb regression.

Call to Action

I encourage you to start a personal journal where you can write about the challenges you are facing. To guide you in discovering potential influences from your past lives, I'm sharing a template that will help you reflect on different areas of your life.

Self-Reflection Template

1. Do you feel an unexplained attraction or aversion to certain cultures?
(Examples: Chinese, Indian, European, American, Japanese, Egyptian, Greek)

____

____

2. What types of food do you love? Any particular foods you strongly dislike?
(Examples: Indian, Thai, Chinese, Continental, Mexican)

____

____

____

3. What is your favourite style of dressing?
(Examples: Ethnic, Traditional, Western)

____

____

4. Which countries would you love to visit? Which countries do you dislike?

____

____

5. Do you have a preference for any particular type of building or architecture?
(Examples: Indian, Victorian, Egyptian)

____

____

____

6. Have you ever experienced déjà vu—feeling as if you've been in a place or situation before?

____

____

7. Is there a historical event that fascinates you and makes you want to learn more about it?
(Examples: World War I or II, freedom struggles)

____

____

8. Do you feel a special connection to certain animals or birds?

____

____

9. What type of climate do you enjoy the most and why?

____

____

10. What was your favourite childhood game?

____

____

11. Which occupations are you naturally drawn to?

____

____

____

12. Do you have any talents or abilities that seem to come to you spontaneously, without formal learning?

____

____

____

13. How would you describe your personality traits?

____

____

____

14. What fears or phobias do you carry?

____

____

____

15. What kind of books, films, or plays are you most interested in?

____

____

____

16. Do you experience recurring dreams? If so, what are they about?

____

____

____

17. Do you have any scars or birthmarks on your body?

____

____

____

18. Which gender are you most comfortable around?

____

19. Do you instantly like or dislike some people upon meeting them?

____

____

20. What are your favourite colours, and are there any colors you can't stand?

____

____

21. Detail all the illnesses you've experienced.

____

____

22. What attitude do you carry towards your illness, and why?

____

____

23. Do you believe your illness serves a purpose in your life? If so, what might that purpose be?

____

____

24. Do you think certain thoughts, beliefs, or emotional patterns contribute to your illness?

____

____

25. Are you truly committed to healing yourself and moving toward wellness?

____

____

26. List the emotions, fears, and anxieties that overwhelm you.

____

____

____

27. How much effort are you willing to put into overcoming your fears, negative emotions, and phobias?

____

____

____

28. Write down the names of people who have made you feel loved, trusted, and supported. Why do you feel this way about them?

____

____

____

____

29. Write down the names of people who have hurt or disappointed you, causing resentment or anger. In front of each name, describe what they did that led to these feelings.

____

____

____

____

30. Who do you feel most confident around, and why?

____

____

____

31. How many times a week do you practice meditation? And which meditation?

____

____

____

____

32. Are you able to focus for how long during meditation?

____

____

33. What emotions arise during meditation?

____

____

34. Any sensation you feel in your mind and body? Write them.

____

____

35. Do you get any recurring thoughts during meditation?

____

____

36. Did any memory good/ bad arise during Womb Regression? Does it need healing?

____

____

37. Did you integrate the memory for further growth?

____

____

38. How was your experience of womb regression?

____

____

39. Did you feel welcomed in the present life by your parents and other family members?

____

____

A Final Thought: **"Within you, there is a stillness and a sanctuary to which you can retreat at any time and be yourself."**
-   Hermann Hesse

5. STEP 1 – UNDERSTANDING THE ROOT CAUSE

"Healing begins when we acknowledge the roots of our suffering."
- Thich Nhat Hanh

In this chapter, we will explore the first crucial step of healing – identifying the root cause of the problems an individual is facing. Often, these unresolved issues stem from past lives and must be addressed to achieve emotional, mental, physical, and spiritual healing.

Uncovering the root cause offers clarity, revealing that its connection to the past life may manifest as fear, phobia, anxiety, stress, physical pain, illness, or recurring patterns and habits that disturb us in the present. To better understand how these root causes affect our present lives, let's look at the following case histories:

Case history 1- Fear and trust issue

Shruti always had a recurring fear of losing her business. She feared and would not trust anyone. She had a major trust issue. When taken into a past life, the root cause of her fear was found coming from a past life, where her business partner cheated and she lost her business because of him.

After finding the truth, with understanding and integration, her anxiety and fear diminished gradually. Then onward she started doing well in her business. Now she is a successful businesswoman in her field. She started trusting people and has had some collaborations that took her to greater heights.

Case history 2 - recurring massive pain healed

Raman, a 26 years old young man was facing recurring pain in his chest. He tried all conventional medicine but none worked. Doctors couldn't find the root cause of his pain. The pain was getting terrible day by day and while lying on the bed, was unbearable.

One of his friends, who knew about past life regression suggested, that he should take the help of past life regression therapy. When Raman came to me, he was in too much pain and appeared very tired. He looked much more than his age due to his medical condition. For him, this was the last resort to be freed from the pain.

The very next day I regressed him and the memory from a past life surfaced, in which he was lying down and doing weight lifting above the chest. The weight was quite heavy and he lost control. The entire weight fell onto his chest and due to bleeding and massive pain, he became unconscious and died there and then on the dumbbell bench. He saw his soul leaving the body; it was white in color.

I made him watch with detachment, so that he would not feel the pain during the session. Insight came, the root cause was revealed and with integration his pain diminished, and profound healing took place. Now he is enjoying a pain-free life towards wellness.

Case History 3 - Guilt from the past healed

Robin, a 50-year-old man, came to me along with his wife, because of the feeling of being a victim at home and in the workplace. His wife Mary told me, that she is tired of him since he doesn't make any decisions about family and children. Ultimately, she has to become the man of the house. But when she makes decisions, he feels that she is commanding him and feels suppressed and victimized.

When regressed, he saw himself as a woman in her fifties named Martha of Spanish origin living off the south coast of America in the 18th century with her husband Robert and daughter Julia. She lost her husband due to a long illness and now wanted to come back to Spain and spend the rest of her life where she belonged, with her daughter Julia.

Martha and Robert loved Julia a lot, being an only child born after many years of their marriage. Robert while breathing his last asked Martha to take care of Julia.

Julia was not happy with Martha's decision to go back to Spain as she was born and brought up in the US. Both mother and daughter fought over this issue. Later Martha decided to leave Julia in the US and stay in Spain. They agreed to keep visiting each other. After a month Martha received the devastating news that Julia had lost her life in a road accident. She went into guilt mode, feeling that she had lost her daughter because of her decision to leave the US to settle in Spain.

The root cause of the current problem had come from this particular past life where Martha's decision had put her in guilt. Therefore, Robin was scared to make any decisions at home and in his workplace. On regression, in a spirit world he met Julia who told him that she had lost her life since her time on earth was over and she had to take birth in another life in another place, and it was not because of Martha (Robin) that she had lost her life.

This brought great insight that it was not his fault. With this understanding, he healed himself from guilt with integration and reframing (through the NLP technique). After that, he started making decisions of his own, received back his power, and no longer felt victimized.

This brings an understanding of how the root causes of incidents in our past lives trouble us in our present life and often paralyze us.

Most of the time when relationship problems are the root cause; there is unresolved karma from the past life with the person one is facing.

From these cases it's not difficult to understand that

root cause is a key to unlocking the secrets of the past to heal the present.

Guided Regression – A Step-by-Step Process to Explore Past Lives

Guided regression is a powerful tool to explore past lives, typically done through progressive relaxation, guided by a trained practitioner. If you'd like to attempt it yourself, consider recording the steps in your voice, using a calm and soothing tone.

Later, you can listen to it and follow along. However, for the first experience, I strongly suggest you seek the guidance of a trained practitioner. This way, you'll get a better understanding of how the process works and how to use the right tone and commands when guiding yourself through a regression.

Find a quiet place

Where you will feel relaxed and comfortable and will not be disturbed by anyone. Switch off your mobile and keep it away. Inform family members to not disturb you unless you come out of the place. Allow yourself to focus on the process.

Set an intention

Setting an intention is a must before going for the session. Otherwise, you may enter into any life which will not give you any clue.

Example: suppose you want to find out the root cause

of your problem in your relationship with your father. Giving an intention connects me only with the life from where the origin of my problem with my father originated. Repeat this intention three to four times when starting the process.

Relaxing and Breathing

Lie down in a comfortable position and focus on your breath. Breathe in and breathe out... five to six times, and gradually feel relaxation in the whole body.

Bring your attention to your toes; tighten the toe's muscles, and relax. Now move your attention to your legs and tighten the legs and release; next move to your knees and thighs, tighten and release, your pelvic area - tighten and release, lower abdomen and lower back - tighten and release; stomach and middle back- again tighten and release. Move attention to your chest and pectoral area and your shoulder blades- tighten and then release.

Move to your arms and tighten and release. Now bring your attention to the neck, tighten and release. Bring your attention to your jaws and teeth and relax them. If your teeth are clenched, unclench them. Relax your muscles around your eyes and eyebrows and relax. Tighten your forehead and relax. Relax your mind. If there is any unstopped chatter, stop and focus on relaxation. Relax your head and feel the relaxation all over the body.

At this point, I will count from 3 to 1 and you will double the relaxation in your body. 3.. 2... 1... Now your relaxation has doubled. (The dots in between each count are a little pause. The longer the dots, the more the pause and vice versa).

Once again, I will count from 3 to 1, and with the count, relax your muscles. 3...2...1..., a thousand times more and you will feel each and every part of your body is relaxed and in comfort.

At this point, you are only attracted to my voice which will increase your relaxation more and more and will respond. All the outside noises will only help you go to a deeper layer of relaxation.

Now I am going to count from 5 down to 1, and on each count, you can relax more and more. Let the relaxation increase throughout your entire body...becoming relaxed ...5 more relaxed... 4... Very comfortable and relaxed...3. More and more relaxed... 2... even more relaxed in your entire body...1... now every nerve, every muscle. Every tissue, every cell in your body has relaxed... more and more relaxed......

Every muscle, every tissue, every nerve, every fibre every cell in your body is in the ultimate state of relaxation.... As you completely let go, loosen up and relax more and more.... Feeling very free and relaxed.... Your body feels perfectly comfortable... all discomforts are now gone from your body... all your organs and all your glands are functioning perfectly now. Your whole body is relaxed and functioning perfectly......

And now that you have increased your awareness...... allow yourself to deepen the state of relaxation, and go to your favourite place, this can be a place where you enjoy nature or could be your favourite healing place…. Allow yourself to be there… allow all your senses to be open to all the things there… look around, become aware of the textures and colours of the flora and fauna around you…become aware of the smells, the smell that seems to permeate this special place…. With every breath that you take, with every sense of this place, feel yourself going deeper and deeper into relaxation… feel the ground under your feet, so with every step that you take you release more and more bodily tension….

Crossing the bridge of time

Now imagine or visualize yourself walking across the field in your favourite place… feel the cool breeze blowing …. Feel the fragrance coming from all around…. Listen to the chirping of birds……hear the gentle voice of the river flowing nearby….

Approach the river now…. Once you reach the river you will find a bridge across it…. You can see the fog all around as well as on the bridge…you can't see the other side due to fog…. Only a few steps you see in front of you…. Climb onto the bridge and start taking steps…. With each step you take on this bridge, allow yourself to approach one of your past lives where the root cause for your problem lies…. (Repeat the intention in your mind, which life you want to visit.

Example: connect me to the past life from where all my problems in my relationship with my father came from in present life).

In a moment I shall be counting down from 10 to 0. When I reach count 0 you will step down the bridge…. And

…. Enter into one of your past lives…. Which holds the root cause of your problem….

10…9…over the bridge of time………

8…… 7…. Keep walking over the bridge of time.

6…… 5…. You can see the fog now…….

4…… 3…As you are walking over the bridge the fog is becoming thicker and thicker…. You are not able to see the far end of the bridge…. You are able to see only a few steps in front of you……

2… Now the fog is beginning to clear…… Everything seems clearer now…….

1…… you are almost on the other side of the bridge…

By the count of zero (0) you will step down the bridge and enter into a past life where the root cause of your issue lies…….

You can relive and remember everything….

0…… Now the fog has completely cleared and you have stepped into another body, another lifetime…another experience…….

Look down at your feet what kind of footwear you are wearing?

Look at yourself and answer if you are a male or female.

Look at your skin colour and tell the tone of your body colour.

How old are you?

Which place are you, indoor or outdoor?

Try to look around and tell if it's day or night.
Is there anyone with you?

What type of dress are you wearing? Pay attention to all the details.

Go to important, significant moments of this life.......by going backward and forward in time......see what you see.... Feel what you feel.... Hear what you hear....

Tell me about your family and your profession.......

See about your relationship with family and others.

Is there anyone in the present life you feel is from this life?

Final Moments and Understanding

Now progress to the last day of that lifetime and observe what happens with you.

What's the colour of your soul?

Are you alone or is someone with you in your last moments?

Now detach yourself from that scene.... And float above the scene...... What did you learn from that life?

What's the root cause of your problem attached to that life troubling you in the present life?

What happened after your death? Who is guiding you after death state?
Move ahead into the spirit world. Receive a message or

guidance from your spirit guide.

Returning to the Present

In a moment I am going to count from 1 to 5……….

with the count of five, you will be wide awake, relaxed, and rejuvenated.

1…2…3…4…5… now you can open your eyes…. Wide awake…. Feeling better than ever before….

First Ever Session Kindly Taken from a Trained Practitioner to Understand Better.

Reflection on What You Have Learnt and Journal

Try to connect the patterns/habits from the present life to the past life for your root cause. Reflect on the images and intuition you experienced. Journal everything you experienced to get insight.

Precautions

Don't get up immediately after the session to avoid falling. Some people feel a bit dizzy after the session.

Most of the time people feel heavy for a while after a session.

Having a glass of water/ cup of tea or coffee will refresh you and you will feel more relaxed.

There Are Many Techniques for Accessing Past Life

Memories...

Different people respond to different techniques.

Hypnosis for Past Life Regression

Some therapists use hypnosis for quicker access to clients' minds.

Past life through reiki

With this technique, you can explore yourself if you do self-reiki or you can take the help of a therapist. This technique is used to clear the blocked energies, from the energy fields as well as by cleaning and balancing all seven chakras.

Very easily, one can find a blocked chakra by placing a hand above the chakra to find whether energy is flowing or not. The sensation in your hands gives you an indication of the flow of energy.

While healing, one may explore past life memories also. This will give you a better understanding of how each chakra is connected to different body parts, and you will get the idea of which area in your life is not working properly. By cleaning and balancing one can balance the chakra. Clean and balance all the seven chakras to attain perfect health at all levels.

The power of dreams in revealing a past life...

If you are experiencing a recurring dream of a specific place, person/s or incident and it feels more vivid, real and emotionally intense while having nothing to do with your present life, in that case, it's related to your past life.

Keep a dream journal to track and interpret these memories. Last thing before going to sleep, set an intention to uncover the past life related to your recurring dream. This will be uncovered over time. The subconscious mind will reveal what you need to know.

The techniques, shared above are used by practitioners. Individuals can explore their past lives with the help of anyone they feel comfortable with.

Keep practicing from time to time to resolve different issues that have no solution in present life, for better health- mentally, emotionally, physically and spiritually.

By reflecting on past lives, one can understand the patterns affecting their present, overcome fear, and use the knowledge to shape their current life. This self-awareness leads to emotional freedom, better relationships, and living a life aligned with the soul's purpose.

Call to Action

Journaling helps you to find, the core issue so keep journaling about past life memories/patterns/habits/ emotional triggers and their connection in the present life.

Journal the messages or guidance received by your spirit guide.

____

____

____

____

Write down a recurring dream you are getting, which has no connection with the present.

____

____

____

Once the subconscious reveals what you need to know, you write it down.

____

____

____

What is the root cause you saw troubling you in the present life?

____

____

____

Affirmations to use daily–

"I am willing to explore the depths of my past lives to heal my present."

"With every memory, I gain wisdom and release pain from my soul's journey."

"I trust that the lessons from my past lives are guiding me towards healing and growth."

"I honour my past lives and the experiences that shaped my soul." "Each past life memory I uncover brings me closer to emotional freedom and peace."

> **"The past is not a place to get stuck but a treasure trove of lessons for the present."**
> *- Michael Newton.*

6. STEP 2 – HEALING AND RELEASING

Healing begins with letting go of the past and embracing the possibility of a better future.
- Marianne Williamson

In the previous chapter, you learnt how to explore past lives and uncover the root causes of present issues. Now, I will take you on a journey through the next essential step—healing—using various techniques.

Once the root cause is identified during a past life regression session, the next step is to release all the emotional, physical and mental pain connected to that trauma. It's about letting go of the baggage you've carried throughout your lifetimes and finding emotional freedom, peace, and spiritual growth in your present life.

In this chapter, we will explore practical healing techniques such as forgiveness, emotional release, and energy healing. By learning these processes, you can free yourself from the pain, trauma, and limitations caused by unresolved past-life issues, allowing you to live a more complete, fulfilling life.

Understanding the need for healing and releasing —

During the session, unresolved issues from the past surface, and these need to be taken care of to free emotional and negative energies. This can be anything– fear, guilt, anger or resentment.

These energies of unresolved issues manifest as pain in the body, and mental problems, leading to mental blocks, and can even hamper one's growth. By resolving these, one can bring balance and lead a happy life.

Common Effects of Unhealed Past Life Wounds

If past wounds remain unhealed, they often repeat themselves in the present as recurring habits or patterns.

Emotional wounds

If not healed emotionally, energy gets blocked and hampers one's growth at all levels of life.

Chronic Physical Pains

These pains from past life accidents, wounds or infections can bring massive physical pains without finding any reason in the present life. Most of the time, clients avail past life sessions when doctors are unable to trace the source of the pain and just give medication and the pains subside temporarily, not heal.

Relationship issues

Unresolved issues of relationships from past life can be challenging and can create dysfunctional relationships in the present life. Most of the time you repeat the same patterns and habits you carry from past life.

Healing Techniques

There are many different techniques people can follow for release and healing. Let's explore some powerful methods that I have found transformative for my clients.

Forgiveness exercise

Forgiveness is a powerful exercise for letting go of past karma. I prefer to use it on my clients. This technique can release unresolved issues like hurt, betrayal, and many more conflicts in relationships to bring harmony to present life.

Self-forgiveness practice

Sit or lie down in a quiet place and reflect on past or present life experiences where you felt shame, guilt or regret for what you did in your past or present life.

Follow these steps

Place your hand on your chest and say out loud.

"I forgive myself for any harm I may have caused. I release

all the guilt/ shame /regret and allow love and healing to flow in my heart.

Repeat this affirmation several times, till you feel the release and feel lighter and contended.

Forgiving others

I forgive (name of the person you need to forgive) wholeheartedly for the harm (name the harm) caused to me by him/her. I allow love and healing to flow in my heart and I direct the love and healing to flow to (name of the person) also.

Breath works for emotional release.

Sit comfortably and focus on your breath.

Begin to deepen your breath by inhaling with the count of four and exhaling with the count of six.

After a few minutes shift to a circular breathing pattern - inhale deeply from your nose and exhale from your mouth without pause.

Bring the intention in your mind what you want to release– guilt/ shame/ regret.

After a few breaths, allow your emotions to surface. During this, you may feel like laughing/ crying or maybe your body starts trembling. Don't get scared and allow the release to take place as these are the signs of emotional energies from past lives for complete healing.

Keep repeating till a sense of peace and calmness is felt.

Releasing by crying

People cry when they feel overwhelmed by their emotions. By crying you can release emotional baggage that you have been carrying for a long time. By crying, catharsis takes place at all the levels. By crying you can shed the load and release negative energies and emotions.

Both above-mentioned techniques are used to bring healing during past life sessions once the root cause is found.

I practice every day, gratitude in the morning, and forgiveness before sleeping.

Reiki healing

Energy healing is used to release emotional blocks as well as physical problems.

You can clean, heal, and balance by reiki energy to remove blockages in aura and chakras.

I have already described earlier how to recognise a blocked chakra by placing your hand above it and if energy is not flowing from your hand or the energy flow is too fast, it means the chakra is blocked.

By focussing on a chakra in a meditative state, memories from past life surface and reveal the root cause. Then and there you itself can heal the chakra by realising the root cause and thereby releasing negative energy. This will allow the chakra to clean, heal and balance.

There are seven chakras related to different parts of

the body. Healing the particular chakra heals all the organs and body parts related to that chakra.

For example,

The Root Chakra (first chakra)

Located at the base of the spine and associated with the colour red, it often gets blocked due to deep fears related to survival, usually stemming from past traumas. When the root chakra is blocked, it can manifest in several ways:

Physical issues like problems in the legs, feet, tailbone, rectum, immune system, male reproductive organs or prostate glands.

Emotional struggles such as anxiety, depression, fear, panic attacks, worry, overthinking, nightmares, anger and low self-esteem.

Mental patterns of poor focus, pessimism and a consistently negative outlook.

Feeling stuck or unable to take action, rushing from task to task with no energy, and a sense of lethargy and distractibility.

The Sacral Chakra (second chakra)

This is closely linked to our desires for sexual and social fulfillment and emotional intelligence. Situated in the lower belly, just below the navel, and in the lumbar spine, it is associated with the colour orange and the element of water. The sacral chakra, or Svadhisthana, governs:

Pleasure: It's the centre of our emotions and feelings, inviting us to embrace joy.

Creativity: This chakra is where our creative energy flows and thrives.

Freedom: It's all about fun, freedom, and flexibility in life.

Sexuality: The sacral chakra helps us express our sexual needs and desires openly.

When this chakra is blocked, we lose touch with these aspects of life, feeling disconnected from joy, creativity, and personal freedom.

The Manipura Chakra

Also known as the solar plexus or third chakra, it is all about personal power, self-esteem and the ability to manifest your desires and achieve your goals. A blocked Manipura chakra can lead to:

Digestive problems such as indigestion, heartburn, bloating, constipation and irritable bowel syndrome. Other issues could include pancreatitis, diabetes, arthritis, stomach ulcers and liver-related concerns.

Emotionally, it shows up as low self-confidence, insecurity, doubt, mistrust, unhealthy relationships, lack of motivation, and difficulty in setting boundaries.

Physically, you might experience fatigue, low energy, skin issues like acne, or even dermatitis.

Heart Chakra

Moving upwards, an imbalanced Heart Chakra can make you feel unworthy of love or unable to trust yourself or others. You may also experience physical signs like poor circulation, high or low blood pressure, or stiffness in your chest, shoulders, and upper back. When this chakra is unlocked, you begin to flow with love, face situations with courage, and connect to your higher self.

Throat chakra A blocked Throat Chakra can make it hard to express your true thoughts and feelings, leading to misunderstandings and emotional conflicts in relationships. You might experience physical symptoms like a sore throat, stiff neck, headaches, or even a tight jaw. Emotionally, this blockage might show up as biting your tongue, avoiding conflicts, or even habitual lying.

Third Eye Chakra (Ajna chakra)

When the Third Eye Chakra (Ajna chakra) is blocked, it manifests as:

Headaches, blurred vision, sensitivity to light, and other eye-related issues.

Indecision, confusion, lack of focus, depression, anxiety, and mood swings.

A sense of disconnection from your intuition, lack of spiritual awareness, and even sleep problems like insomnia.

Crown Chakra (seventh chakra)

Lastly, when the Crown chakra (seventh chakra) is blocked, you may experience:

Poor coordination, headaches, dizziness, sensitivity to light, brain fog, and tension in the neck or jaw.

Emotionally, it can lead to feeling disconnected from yourself and the world, experiencing confusion, isolation, anxiety, or even an existential crisis.

Overthinking, low self-confidence, and a lack of trust in oneself or others may also arise from this imbalance.

When you release the negative energy from these chakras, the healing of past pains, emotional scars, and traumas occurs. This healing leads to a newfound sense of clarity, emotional freedom, and a lighter, more joyful way of being.

Aura Cleaning

Follow these steps to cleanse your aura:

Visualize a Golden or White Light: Sit comfortably and picture a radiant white or golden light enveloping your body, extending several feet outward in all directions.

Scan for Dark Spots: Mentally scan your aura for any dark or shadowy spots—these are wounds or energy blockages from past or present traumas.

Heal the Aura: Visualize the golden or white light dissolving the dark spots. Allow the light to heal and free you from these negative energies.

Check Your Aura: Once your energy field appears clearer, balanced, and bright, you will feel a sense of lightness and peace. If any dark spots remain, repeat the process until they are fully healed.

To promote balance in your chakras, you can also try:

Yoga postures, such as the sphinx pose, the camel pose, the cat pose, the fish pose, and the chest fly kundalini exercise.

Breathing practices like Pranayam to encourage the flow of energy.

Daily meditation to bring about clarity of mind.

Physical pain removal

Recurring pain without any reason is linked to your past life trauma/ accidents/ wounds.

Find Comfort and Breathe:

Sit or lie down in a comfortable and silent place. Take a deep breath three to four times and bring your attention to the area of the body where you feel pain, stress, anxiety or discomfort.

Visualize Healing Light:

Visualize a light (color) of your own choice on the top of your head and entering your body.

Allow the light to flow into the area of discomfort, pain, anxiety, or stress.

Focus on the area of discomfort and see the colour of light present in that area getting replaced by the light entering your body. (If you see black or gray or some other colour dissolve it with the colour of a healing light.)

Change the Shape:

If you see any shape of that discomfort, change it into another shape of your choice. (suppose you see a rectangular shape, change it to a triangle   circle, or square).

Once the Pain Disappears:

Once it's done you will feel the pain disappearing gradually.

Keep practicing till you feel comfortable, light, and at ease.

Is healing taking place, how to find out

It's important to know whether healing has taken place or not before moving forward to the next step.

Clarity and Perspective:

You will find clarity and a shift in your perspective. One finds a sense of better understanding in the present life.

Physical Relief:

Once healing takes place, all discomfort and pains in your body will disappear.

Emotional Balance:

Emotionally you will be more balanced and at peace after you shed the baggage you have carried for so long.

Improved Relationships:

By releasing past karmas your relationship with your loved ones will become stronger and a new understanding will develop.

Moving Forward with Confidence

Healing is a continuous journey of self-discovery and transformation. It doesn't end with just one session. Keep practicing, keep releasing, and continue to free yourself from the burdens of past lives. This process opens the door to a fulfilling, happy and meaningful life.

Call to Action

Which healing technique did you use, and why?

____

____

____

What was the root cause you healed, and how did you release it?

____

____

____

____

How do you know healing has taken place?

____

____

____

____

Affirmations to Practice

"I release the pain of my past and open myself to healing and love."

"With every breath, I let go of emotional and physical burdens that no longer serve me."

"I forgive myself and others, creating space for peace and freedom in my life."

"I trust the healing process and embrace the release of old traumas."

"My soul is free to heal, grow, and thrive in the present moment."

"In order to heal, we must first forgive, and sometimes the person we need to forgive is ourselves."
- Maya Angelou.

7. STEP 3 – REBUILDING A POSITIVE PRESENT

"The past is behind; learn from it. The future is ahead; prepare for it. The present is here; live it."
Thomas S. Monson.

Living in the Present and Shaping Your Future

In the previous chapter, you learnt how to heal after uncovering past life traumas. Now, we move forward to the third step—creating a positive present and future.

Healing opens the door to new possibilities, but real transformation occurs when we apply the lessons we've learnt to our current lives. This shift brings clarity, allowing us to cultivate new habits, patterns, and a positive mindset. A happy, fulfilling life is not just a dream—it's a reality you can build, step by step, for complete growth in all areas of your life.

How to Process and Integrate Past Life Memories:

Catharsis – Healing on Physical, Mental, and Emotional Levels:

The first step toward healing is catharsis, a deep emotional and physical release.

Physical Catharsis: Relieving bodily symptoms or discomfort tied to past traumas.

Emotional Catharsis: Freeing yourself from the heavy emotional baggage that has weighed you down for too long.

Intellectual Catharsis: Achieving peace of mind by letting go of stress, anxiety, and overthinking.

Detachment from Past Memories:

The second step is learning to detach from the past. Once you realize the past is over, you can find peace. With this understanding, you can move forward, unburdened by what once held you back.

Remember that **your soul is eternal**, constantly changing forms across different lifetimes. It's infinite, multi-dimensional, and not limited by your past experiences.

Transforming the Past into Wisdom:

The third step is to take those past experiences and

transform them into valuable wisdom.

Re-framing (an NLP technique) helps you see old memories from a fresh perspective.

Re-scripting allows you to rewrite the story of your past in a way that feels empowering and acceptable.

Look at the past as a **teacher**, guiding you toward new learning and personal growth. This shift will help you keep progressing to greater heights.

Changing Your Belief System:

To fully let go of the past, you need to change the beliefs tied to those old stories.

This involves creating a new narrative—one that supports your present and future self, rather than holding you back.

By rewriting your inner story, you reshape the beliefs that define your reality.

Steps to follow after Integration: Self-awareness:

Practicing self-awareness helps in continuously keeping a check on your thoughts and the sensations you feel in your body. If any past negative memory resurfaces once again, then this needs attention. You can change them with the energy healing you learnt in the previous chapter. Choose positivity to navigate towards a better life.

Clean your energy every day to release any stress or

situations you face in present-day life to keep yourself balanced and calm. This prepares you for the challenges you face in the future with ease.

Mindfulness:

Become a champion of your life by dealing with your emotions with calmness with the practice of mindfulness. Staying in the present helps us to enjoy everything happening around us at that point in time. Don't dwell in the past, it will only hurt you. Living with mindfulness helps us to keep away old patterns and habits.

Kabat-Zinn adds to his definition of mindfulness by describing it as "awareness that arises through paying attention, on purpose, in the present moment, non-judgmentally."

Spend time with yourself to watch the sensations in your body whether they are negative or positive. This will keep you in the present moment.

Cultivate the habit of gratitude:

Pay thanks to the universe for things you are grateful for in your life, big or small. This will shift your mind from scarcity to abundance.

Develop positive habits and patterns:

This will form the foundation for a healthy mind, body, and spirit. These new habits will keep you grounded to maintain emotional freedom, received through healing.

Self-compassion:

Be compassionate with yourself and appreciate your healing journey. Don't be harsh on yourself in the desire to be perfect. Just allow yourself to evolve and grow.

Create healthy boundaries:

Create healthy boundaries in your relationships to construct a beautiful present with family and friends. This keeps you balanced emotionally and physically. Boundaries protect from falling back to past habits and patterns.

Creating healthy communication:

Create healthy communication to avoid confusion. Healing helps us become more open to others, helping to connect with others easily.

Mind your environment:

It's also important to take care of the environment you live in. What you surround yourself with has a lot of impact on who you are. If your surroundings are positive with the right state of mind, then people, objects, and spaces uplift and inspire you to transform.

Spending time in nature helps to rejuvenate and create positive energy within.

Emotional sustenance:

You need to sustain your emotional quotient, which has become balanced through healing through past life sessions and clearing traumas and negative energies. In everyday life, due to stress and anxiety, our emotions can fluctuate and bring back old wounds by triggers from the present.

Keep journaling:

For emotional clarity keep track of your healing journey. Write these emotions with a detachment so as to not get overwhelmed. This will bring clarity to the field in which one needs to work.

Physical activity:

Doing yoga along with breath exercises helps to release endorphins which keeps you motivated towards positivity and keeps you aligned with continuous healing.

Create a vision for a positive future and set goals to achieve:

Positive intentions for your future goals will keep you aligned with your true values and desires. This helps to connect with your higher self to receive guidance towards building a positive future. Personal growth helps you to balance and grow emotionally, mentally, physically, and spiritually all the time.

Create healthy relationships with people around you based on respect, clarity, love, mutual understanding, and mutual growth.

Find out the purpose of your life. Find out whether or not what you love to do is aligned with the purpose.

Visualize a Positive Future:

Keep practicing a simple visualization to manifest whatever you want in life. Visualize yourself in the future, living your ideal dream.

The correct way to manifest is not to visualize and think that I will have all these in the future. Instead, visualize what you have already achieved and enjoy the same. Whenever you want to manifest anyting, feel the sensations of that manifestation in your body; this creates a neural pathway connecting your mind and body. Practice it every day for fifteen to twenty minutes. Feel the emotions and hold the vision in your mind to focus on the sense of peace and fulfilment.

Spiritual Transformation:

Once healing has taken place, you can connect with your higher self, spirit guides and divine forces to receive messages for personal growth.

If you love to pray, then pray every day to be connected with divine forces and be full of gratitude for their guidance in your life.

Maintain your transformation:

-by choosing and practicing new habits and patterns to support you in your ongoing journey. Keep reflecting from time to time and be ready to incorporate changes if required for your personal growth. This will keep you aligned with your purpose, growth and intentions.

Never stop learning:

Keep growing by learning through books, videos, workshops, journals as well as from your own experiences and those of others. Always be open to learning new techniques of healing which will improve your life and provide a breakthrough. The door for improvement comes from seeking opportunities for self-growth.

Call to Action:

Did catharsis occur at all levels? What was your experience?

____

____

____

Were you able to detach from memories and find peace?

____

____

____

What technique helped you transform your understanding?

____

____

____

How do you now see yourself as the creator of your past, present, and future?

____

____

____

Which belief from the past did you change for a better present?

____

____

____

Write down your growth on your spiritual path.

____

____

____

What personal changes have you made for growth in your life's journey?

____

____

What messages, guidance, or insights have you received from your masters or guides? Are you following them?

____

____

____

What new habit or belief system will you integrate into your present life?

____

____

____

How has your perspective shifted after healing from memories?

____

____

____

Affirmations to rebuild a positive present:

"I am free from the past, and I am creating a positive and abundant present."

"Every day, I choose to cultivate habits that support my healing and growth."

"I am aligned with my highest potential and purpose."

"My future is bright, and I am worthy of peace, love, and happiness."

"I embrace my healing journey and integrate its lessons into my everyday life."

"I create and nurture a life that reflects my inner peace and well-being."

"The best way to predict your future is to create it."
- Abraham Lincoln

8. DIVING DEEPER INTO THE PROCESS

"To heal is to touch with love that which was previously touched by fear."
- Stephen Levine

In the previous chapters, you have experienced and learnt how to find the root cause in the first step, heal yourself in step two, and learn integration in step three.

This chapter will dive into the deeper layers of past lives to find the root cause. Sometimes the root cause comes from many lives and becomes a pattern that can't be dealt with by exploring just one past life.

Rather we need to visit all of those lives and for this, we need advanced techniques to enter deeper layers in many lives one by one, to find the root cause, and to heal. This needs many sessions to explore. You can't visit all of them at once especially if the trauma is complex and doesn't heal after one or two regressions.

If the trauma comes from many lives you need to get your sessions from trained practitioners for better insight to find the root cause. Self-healing can't help you dive deeper and connect all the past lives.

Understanding deeper layers of trauma

One session is not sufficient if the trauma surfacing in the present life is deep-rooted, and needs many sessions of intervention. Wounds from many lives, some memories twine together and surface as trauma. These intertwined unresolved issues need separate exploration.

Fear, anxiety, depression, self-sabotage and relationship issues are emotional issues manifesting in present life as patterns and it is difficult to understand from where they originate.

To access these deeper layers, prolonged guided meditation or visualization is used to explore the subconscious and superconscious mind.

Hypnosis is preferred by healers to explore deeper layers in a short period, allowing clients to bypass the conscious mind without any obstruction, into many lives one after another to discover the emotional trauma disturbing the present life.

In Prolonged visualization techniques, clients have to go for deep visualization for a longer period; to experience the series of experiences they get in those lives to find the connection between past life trauma and present life patterns in multiple lives.

Energy healing by Reiki is also a powerful tool to heal by removing blocked energy and allowing healing to take place at the cellular and energy levels to create wellness. This not only helps to understand the cause but also brings healing by integration and releases trauma from all levels of the body for complete healing.

Following case histories will give you a better perspective, of understanding when the root cause is deep-rooted and intertwined and creates trauma in the present life.

Case history 1

This is the case history of 40-year-old Rakesh who came to me to find a reason for being stuck in his relationships with his mother and wife. He found it difficult to balance both relationships and started avoiding situations, due to which his married life suffered a lot.

In business too, he made losses. He was also suffering from frequent back and leg pain. He went for conventional medicine and massages but this didn't release his pain. He wanted to explore his past life to get rid of his pattern and recurring pain.

When taken, first through womb regression and then into past life regression, to find the root cause of present suffering, he easily slipped into the past life of a Gorilla. He had been resting below a tree when an earthquake came, and he found himself trapped under the tree and his lower body was injured badly and he died.

He then slipped into another life where he saw himself as a young pilot named James, in England in 1928. He saw that he was getting ready in a gray uniform to go to war. In war, his plane crashed and fell in the jungle. His lower body got stuck in the plane wreck and he died in the jungle. He saw two more people who were with him, dying in the crash.

For a while, he slipped into the life of a Tiger and saw his present-life mother as a yogi who had tamed this tiger in that life. The tiger had died while following the Yogi into the deep waves of the sea. His learning from this life was that he should always be alert as life is an unending flow of ups and downs (waves).

Then he slipped into another life ; that of a soldier named Timothy in a war in 1535. He saw himself as an Anglo-Saxon, wearing a horn and animal skin holding a sword and shield to proceed to war in a boat. During the war, his fast-moving boat hit another boat and was damaged badly and he was stuck inside. He struggled to come out of the boat but he was trapped for days, and as his legs started rotting, he finally died with the thought that life has a purpose and he was to live and die only for his country.

Immediately again, he slipped into the life of an Alligator enjoying the warmth of the sun on a winter morning when a volcano erupted and he got stuck in the molten lava which took his life.

Gradually after getting insight and experiencing all the past life memories it was the time to bring him back to the present life for healing and integration.

Repeatedly getting stuck in different lives without action had created a pattern in the present life, due to which he was not able to do anything. The session brought in him a lot of insight and he realized that the pattern has come from many past lives and that he needs to change the pattern with healing.

Watching a regularly dying body, stuck in different situations in different lives brought understanding and healing in him gradually, and the pain from his back and legs disappeared over the period.

The message received from the Yogi in the tiger's life was to be alert during the ups and downs in life, which made him realize that he needed to make changes for a better life and for his relationship with his wife.

From the experience of being submerged in water with a yogi and losing his life in the tiger's life, he also learnt to recognize his own power and not to blindly follow anyone.

He incorporated all these learnings in life and the breakthrough took place in his life. His relationships became better once he took charge of his life. His business bloomed towards growth. He is living a happy, healthy and fulfilled life with his family.

Case history - 2

Anita, a 35-year-old woman, had been struggling with unexplained anxiety, recurring nightmares, and a consistent fear of abandonment. Despite numerous therapies, she couldn't find relief. Her relationships were unstable, and she often felt disconnected from herself.

Seeking deeper healing, Anita took past life regression therapy from me. During the sessions, it was revealed that her fears were from multiple past lives that she had lived.

In her first life in ancient Egypt, Anita was a woman who lost her family in a tragic event. The overwhelming grief and abandonment carried forward into her current life, creating anxiety.

In her second life in medieval Europe, she was a healer betrayed by her close companions, which led to her death. This experience brought deep distrust, making it hard for her to maintain relationships in her current life.

In a third life, she lived in a tribal society. Anita was left alone after a plague wiped out her community. The fear of isolation and abandonment became deep-rooted in her soul's journey.

Through multiple sessions she gained insight from these past traumas. I guided her through releasing the emotional baggage carried from those lives. As she integrated the lessons learnt, her nightmares stopped, and her anxiety began to ease.

Anita learnt to trust again, not only others but also herself. She developed healthier relationships and found a sense of peace that had eluded her for years. With each step in her healing journey, she embraced the understanding that her past lives no longer controlled her present.

Her life transformed as she integrated these lessons,

allowing her to live more fully, free from the emotional traumas of her past. The healing process improved her mental and emotional well-being and brought harmony to her personal and professional life.

Practical Insights and Techniques for Healing

Exploring these cases of past life healing allows us to gain deeper insight into how the process works. It shows us that healing isn't just about understanding, but about integration—taking what we learn and applying it to our current lives for lasting change. This understanding should encourage you to consider past life regression or self-healing for your own journey.

Here are some advanced techniques to help with integration and create long-lasting changes in your life:

Reframing through Visualization: If you're struggling with a difficult relationship, for example, with your mother, visualize a healthier relationship with her with confidence and strength. Make sure you add lots of emotions to it to connect emotionally with your mind and body and feel the sensations in your body while having an emotional relationship with Mom.

Self-Talk: To empower yourself with self-talk, replace negative thoughts with positive ones.

Chakra and Aura Cleansing: Keep cleansing your aura and balancing your chakras through daily Reiki healing or energy work. This helps maintain a state of emotional, mental and physical balance.

Daily Affirmations: Affirmations are powerful for reinforcing new beliefs and behaviors. Here are a few you can practice daily to create a positive state of mind:

"I am free from the past and fully embrace my present."

"I trust in the abundance of the universe and welcome success in all areas of my life."

"I release all fear and live with courage and confidence."

"I am worthy of love, respect, and abundance."

"I am in control of my destiny and create a positive future."

Call to Action

I encourage you to journal your healing journey.

Write down your emotions, patterns, and any negativity that surfaces after your sessions. Reflect on whether further sessions may be needed, and consult with a therapist if necessary.

____

____

____

____

What is the advice you received from a therapist?

____

____

____

____

Advice from a Therapist

My clients keep consulting me, whenever required. They practice mindfulness and forgiveness on a daily basis for continuous healing and integration for a balanced life of happiness, towards growth.

Set clear intentions and practice to achieve whatever you wish to. Explore freedom from the bondage of pain, anxiety, and physical ailments. Your healing is the key to your freedom in life. Embrace freedom without delay.

Intention Setting for Deeper Healing

Here are a few intentions you can set for deeper healing:

"I intend to explore the deeper layers of my past life experiences for lasting healing and growth."

"I choose to release all emotional and physical pain stored in my body from past lives."

"I open myself to the wisdom of my higher self and allow healing to flow freely."

"I am ready to fully integrate my past life healing into my present for lasting transformation."

"I trust in the process of healing and embrace the journey towards a positive future."

Healing can be a long and challenging journey. It's essential to build a support system that includes professional guidance and personal connections. Joining groups of like-minded individuals who are also on a healing path can provide the emotional support and encouragement needed to stay on track.

Group regressions, where individuals explore past life experiences together, can be powerful. These shared healing spaces offer emotional support, and allow participants to witness the healing journeys of others, providing additional layers of insight and validation.

> **"We carry inside us the wonders we seek outside."**
> *-Rumi*

Let that resonate with you, as you continue your journey to healing and self-discovery.

9. HOW TO APPLY THE LESSONS TO EVERYDAY LIFE

*"The greatest glory in living lies not in never falling,
but in rising every time we fall."*
- Nelson Mandela

In the previous chapter, you delved into the profound layers of healing and the techniques to uncover the traumas and pains that have emerged from multiple past lives. You learnt how lessons are woven through experiences and insights by exploring these lives. Now, it's crucial to discover how to apply these invaluable lessons in your present life.

Once you learn the lessons from past lives after the session, if you don't apply them, it's of no use. I will make it easier for you by showing what steps should be taken further –

Consistency is the key to successful health

Continuously practicing will keep you aligned with your goals as well as prepare you for the challenges faced in everyday life. Morning meditation for ten to fifteen minutes will keep you grounded and will prepare you for the positive future you want for yourself, through daily visualization. Practicing affirmations morning and evening will remind you of your strength and resilience to overcome past challenges.

Practice gratitude every day for things you are grateful for. This changes the mindset from scarcity to abundance. Keep your mind calm and keep stress away with breathing exercises. This also helps you to stay in the present moment. Keep reflecting at least once a week on what went right or wrong; how you tackled your challenges and responded to emotional challenges.

Ask yourself how the lessons of this book shaped your responses during challenging situations.

You need to be able to recognize, especially during challenging times, if you fall back into old habits and patterns. Pause and watch what is coming from past life emotional wounds or trauma. Are they here to remind us that something more is to be taken care of? This will make you aware and allow you to heal further. Don't doubt the process; keep moving further in life.

Visualization is a powerful tool whenever you face challenges:

Practice visualization, whenever you face challenging situations. You can reflect on your past life sessions, where you gained back your strength, empowered yourself and integrated the same into the present situation.

Your relationships improve once emotional healing takes place. But sometimes it can be challenging too as others around you are still on the same plane in their unchanged state. In this situation, create healthy boundaries with loved ones and friends. Your experiences will teach you how to maintain that.

Be compassionate towards others, as they have not taken sessions for past life and are still dealing with their own wounds and trauma.

Forgiveness frees you from emotional baggage:

Forgiveness frees you from emotional baggage. First forgive yourself and then others too.

The key is now in your hand. People and situations become weak in front of you as you learn how to maintain emotional balance.

You will have the power to overcome situations with mindfulness and can keep check on your emotions, thoughts and triggers. Mindful listening brings clarity and helps to avoid misunderstandings. Mindful eating makes you enjoy every bite you eat, and gives you flavor of food, smell, and ingredients.

Keep cleaning, healing and balancing your chakras and keep them protected from negative energies. Cleaning the energy field brings good health at all levels. Continuous healing, brings deeper introspection and deeper healing.

Be open to learn new lessons coming your way, in the journey of healing. This could be through a new relationship, career challenges or a personal breakthrough. Trust the process of healing and keep moving forward with confidence, courage and strength during difficult situations.

Never shy away during emotional breakdowns. Where you can't manage yourself, seek support without hiding pains and traumas. Take guidance and healing, whenever in a problem.

Build friendships with like-minded individuals:

Make friends with like-minded people or join healing committees, where others' experiences and journeys of healing will support you to understand more and be open. Keep in touch with healers for guidance and more sessions if required. This will help you to become consistent and grounded.

Embrace the learnings from the spiritual guidance received during healing sessions; and find out the purpose of your life. Live with your purpose aligned towards your goals and follow the directions of life.

Don't rush the process; trust in divine timing:

Don't be in a rush, trust divine timing. Things do unfold at the right time, only when you are supposed to know them. Healing continuously takes place and may not be visible immediately but will be revealed in time. Whatever happens, happens for good.

Journal your thoughts, feelings or challenges of life as

well as the breakthroughs after healing. It's a powerful tool for reflection and tracking progress. By this, you will understand your emotional triggers and discover where more healing is required.

Call to Action

I encourage you to journal all your experiences, big or small, and the emotions you're feeling. Write them down with mindfulness, awareness, and consistency.

____

____

____

____

____

____

____

____

Affirmations for Applying Lessons to Everyday Life

"I integrate the lessons of my past healing into every moment of my present."

"I embrace life's challenges as opportunities for continued growth and transformation."

"I maintain emotional balance and respond to life with calm and clarity."

"I am consistent in my healing practices, staying aligned with my highest self."

"I trust the process of life and embrace the journey of healing with patience and grace."

"Healing doesn't mean the damage never existed. It means the damage no longer controls our lives."
– Akshay Dubey

10. WHAT TO DO NEXT

"Every day is an opportunity for a new beginning."
- Dalai Lama

Completing the healing process detailed in this book is a major milestone in your journey of self-discovery and emotional transformation. However, healing is not an endpoint; it's an ongoing journey that requires continuous reflection, growth and action.

After finishing the steps and techniques you've learnt, the next phase is about staying committed to your progress, continuing to explore deeper aspects of self-awareness, and staying open to further healing if necessary. This chapter offers guidance on what to do next, as you embark on this ongoing journey of personal growth and spiritual exploration.

Like life's journey, healing is an ongoing process. If

you stop healing, you will feel stagnant and will attract old emotional patterns and habits. There is a lot you need to explore in deeper layers and advanced healing, for more insight and growth in life. You need to be committed towards self-development and progress. I can bet you once you practice and explore further, you will add much more experiences and insight. Every time you embark on a fresh session, there will be new experiences waiting to reveal more and more.

Be prepared for new challenges coming along your way, while graduating in life. Handling challenges makes you stronger, confident and emotionally balanced. Once we learn to overcome them, a sense of victory comes to us, and we stay prepared for more to come.

Integrating with mindfulness lessons learnt during the healing journey brings more focus, and you get connected with your higher self. You need to be consistent in self-care after the healing sessions. Once you have gained insight, it gives you the power to grow spiritually as per the beliefs you created, and helps to connect with the divine self.

Now you are prepared to adopt more advanced meditation practices - like Ana-Pana-Sati ((breath meditation), and need more attention and focus. Learn more about the spiritual path and techniques and philosophies; open up to new learning, to add more to your knowledge.

Develop a habit of reading. Personally, I am an avid reader, always seeking to expand my understanding. It's a practice that I cherish and highly recommend. Staying connected with your learning and healing practices, and aligning them with your evolving goals, is crucial. As you grow, your goals will naturally change. Flexibility is key.

Time to time, reflect on your journal and check your developments and additions in your habit. New habits and patterns take time to get used to. Stay connected with your intuitions, to stay connected with the self at all levels. This could be your work, finances, relationship, career, health, and more will show in your growth and will bring a sense of fulfillment. I call it spiritual freedom.

With time, you may find new triggers and patterns disturbing you. Go for another session to explore. Some triggers develop with age, also connected with the same age in past lives. Keep checking them, and balance them with the healing techniques you have learnt.

Healing is good for overall development, but at times it can also be mentally or emotionally draining. Because of this, you need to take rest at intervals to protect yourself from burnout. This helps the body to rejuvenate and recharge for further explorations.

Taking a walk in an open area or garden, listening to music, playing some games, exercising or practicing yoga and creative activity is also a form of healing. Bring them into your life and incorporate them in your daily routine.

For diving deeper and evolving, go in for more advanced techniques like Inner Child healing, Shadow work, family counselling and Kundalini healing.

Find a mentor or spiritual guide to navigate and transform in the right direction, quenching your thirst for more answers and insight. Choose someone who resonates well with your beliefs and values, to ensure your alignment with your goal.

Guidance may come from conversation, watching movies or listening to someone. Stay open to these guidance that the universe is sending you, to support you to continue your journey.

Embracing all above with commitment will take you towards growth and transformation along with wisdom, fulfilment, and freedom for a lifetime.

Call to action:

What new techniques have you added to your life for growth?

____

____

How is your spiritual growth taking place, and how is it transforming your life?

____

____

How has this book helped you achieve transformation in different aspects of your life?

____

____

____

____

____

Affirmations to practice:

"I embrace growth and transformation as a lifelong journey."

"I am open to new lessons and healing opportunities that come my way."

"I honour my progress and continue to evolve with love and patience."

"I trust in my inner wisdom and follow the path of my soul's purpose."

"I am deserving of ongoing support and healing as I continue my journey."

"In the process of letting go, you will lose many things from the past, but you will find yourself."
- Deepak Chopra

As you stand at the end of this chapter and the book, remember that your journey doesn't end here—it's just the beginning of a beautiful path toward endless growth and transformation. Healing is like a river, constantly flowing and carving its way through life's obstacles. It may be slow at times, but it never stops. You are that river, and your flow is guided by your inner strength, wisdom, and resilience.

Take a moment to honour the courage it took to embark on this journey. Not everyone is brave enough to face their inner world, and you have done it with grace. You've learnt, grown, and perhaps shed a few tears on the way, but through it all, you've also found pieces of yourself that you may have lost. Hold on to those pieces, for they are the essence of your true self.

Be proud of where you are today, but never stop seeking, and never stop growing. Life will continue to unfold new layers of beauty, challenges, and wisdom. Let each experience enrich your soul, and remind yourself—this journey is uniquely yours. You are stronger than you realize, and the universe is always guiding you toward the light.

Thank you for trusting me to walk with you through these pages. I hope you carry this healing energy forward and inspire others with the same love and strength you've discovered within yourself. Remember, you are never alone on this journey.

Keep healing, keep growing, and keep shining. The best is yet to come.

ABOUT THE AUTHOR

Jaya Kalra is a distinguished healer, visionary artist, and cultural ambassador, renowned for her contributions to holistic wellness and the arts. With over 26 years of experience, she has transformed the lives of thousands through her expertise in therapies such as Reiki, mind-body healing, inner child healing, and neuro-linguistic programming (NLP). Jaya's specialization in Past Life Regression Therapy has been especially impactful, helping individuals uncover deep-rooted traumas and facilitating profound emotional and spiritual healing. Her practice emphasizes addressing the root cause of suffering, allowing people to achieve lasting well-being without medication.

As a life coach and motivational speaker, Jaya is passionate about sharing her knowledge. She reaches a wide audience through her YouTube channel, "It's My Life," and live lectures at institutions and corporations. She covers a range of topics, from mental health to stress-free living, always promoting self-awareness and personal growth.

In addition to her healing work, Jaya is an accomplished artist. She is the founder of Jharokha Art Institution and Chrysalis - The Gallery in Shillong, where she mentors aspiring artists and showcases works from both emerging and established creators. Her art has been exhibited internationally and is celebrated for its vivid colours and deep storytelling.

Jaya's dedication to healing and the arts has earned her numerous accolades, including the prestigious International Reiki Award in 2024. To learn more about her work and services, visit jayakalra.com.